MW00558989

My Spirit-Empowered Day

Harrison House

Shippensburg, PA

A *Sparkling Gems from the Greek*
Guided Devotional Journal

My Spirit-Empowered Day

Rick Renner

Published by Harrison House Publishers
Shippensburg, PA 17257

ISBN 13 TP: 978-1-6675-0210-6

ISBN 13 eBook: 978-1-6675-0211-3

For Worldwide Distribution, Printed in the U.S.A.

1 2 3 4 5 6 7 8 / 28 27 26 25 24

Contents

Preface 7

Day 1   The Holy Spirit — the Great Revealer! 9

Day 2   The Prophetic Ministry of the Holy Spirit 18

Day 3   Jesus and the Holy Spirit 24

Day 4   The Holy Spirit Is Our Seal and Guarantee 32

Day 5   The Holy Spirit Earnestly Yearns for You! 38

Day 6   You Are a Shrine for the Holy Spirit 44

Day 7   The Guiding Ministry of the Holy Spirit 50

Day 8   Don't Put Out the Spirit's Fire! 57

Day 9   The Unseen Power Behind the Throne 63

Day 10   Jesus' Teaching in the Upper Room 68

Day 11   Jesus' Prayer 75

Day 12   The Comforter, Part 1 82

Day 13   The Comforter, Part 2 89

Day 14   The Heavenly Coach 96

Day 15   You're Not a Spiritual Orphan! 103

Day 16   The Holy Spirit Wants to Place a Razor-Sharp Sword in Your Hands 109

Day 17   The Spirit of Truth 116

Day 18   The Glorifying Ministry of the Holy Spirit 123

Day 19   A Spirit of Wisdom and Revelation for You 129

Day 20   The Holy Spirit — a Partner Who Wants to
         Take Responsibility for You in This Life! 135

Day 21   God's Spirit Dwells in You! 142

Day 22   The Permanent Indweller of Your Heart 151

Day 23   The Holy Spirit Is Like Wind 156

Day 24   "Welcome to Your New Home!" 164

Day 25   Machine-Gun Fire and a Cup of Tea! 172

Day 26   A Divine Stream of Supernatural Revelation 179

Day 27   A Guaranteed Way to Infuriate the Holy Spirit! 186

Day 28   What to Do When Your Spirit Is Inwardly Disturbed 193

Day 29   Learning to Follow the Leader 202

Day 30   A Different Kind of Leading 208

Day 31   Do Not Grieve the Holy Spirit! 216

         About the Author 221

Preface

Dear Reader,

When Jesus was preparing to return to Heaven after three years of earthly ministry, He called His disciples together to explain that "another Helper" (John 14:16 *AMP*) would come and would be *inseparably* with and in them to empower them through life. In that statement, Jesus introduced the disciples — *and us* — to the Holy Spirit.

As you begin reading the following 31 devotional entries, I will unveil to you, with insights from the Greek text, the mission of the Holy Spirit in your life. I will share a short teaching and then ask questions to engage your heart and mind as we study together:

- The workings and personality of the Holy Spirit.

- His role in your life as Comforter, Advocate, Counselor, and Strengthener.

- How you can cooperate with Him to walk in power and authority.

As you come into deeper fellowship with the Spirit of God and learn to cooperate with Him fully, you will find yourself walking in the Spirit-empowered life Jesus has prepared for you!

Your friend,

Rick Renner
Moscow, Russia

Day 1

The Holy Spirit — the Great Revealer!

> *But as it is written, Eye hath not seen, nor ear heard, neither have entered into the heart of man, the things which God hath prepared for them that love him. But God hath revealed them unto us by his Spirit....*
>
> — 1 Corinthians 2:9,10

O ver the years, we have received millions of letters from viewers who have written in response to our TV programs. If I were to amass all of those letters and analyze the number-one need that people write to us about, I would have to say it is their desperate desire to know God's will for their lives.

People struggle to know what is right or wrong, what jobs they should or shouldn't take, what school they should attend for higher education, whom they should or should not marry, whether or not to go full time into the ministry

— and on, on, and on. Often well-meaning, misinformed people have told them, "Well, you can't always know God's plan." These misled people even quote First Corinthians 2:9 and use it as an excuse for ignorance. They say, "You know what the Bible says: 'Eye hath not seen, nor ear heard, neither have entered into the heart of man, the things that God hath prepared for them that love him.' You see, even the Bible tells us we can't always know what God has planned for us!"

However, that was *not* the point the apostle Paul was trying to make when he wrote this verse! We cannot use First Corinthians 2:9 as an excuse for *ignorance*. It's true that there was a time long ago under the Old Covenant when it wasn't possible to fully know God's plan as we can know it today. Paul paraphrased from the Old Testament when he said, "...As it is written, Eye hath not seen, nor ear heard, neither have entered into the heart of man, the things which God hath prepared for them..." (*see* Isaiah 64:4). Isaiah was bemoaning the perplexing problem of man's inability to know what God has planned for him. At that time, before the Holy Spirit came to indwell the hearts of people, it was difficult and often impossible to fully discern the things God had planned for each of His children.

Think about how perplexing this problem must have been! God meticulously prepared wonderful, prearranged blessings for His people, but they weren't able to discern these things in advance! The word "prepared" is important in this text, for it is the Greek word *etoimadzo*, which carries the idea of a *readiness* or something that has been *fully prepared*. The use of this word in this verse alerts us to the fact that God has a divine plan for each of our lives and is ready to reveal it! How wonderful to realize that God's plan for us is not happenstance, accidental, or a product of last-minute planning. He has been meticulously working out a plan for our lives since before the foundation of the world. He is the *Great Planner*!

Under the Old Covenant, however, the Holy Spirit didn't reside in the human heart, so people struggled tremendously to find God's predetermined plan for their lives. In their efforts to uncover His will, they sought special, divine signs and even visited prophets of the region in an attempt to find answers and gain God's guidance and direction. Although God had prepared so much for His people, they were blind to much of what had been provided for them because they didn't have the Great Revealer living in their hearts.

How I wish I could say that it was different today, but most modern Christians live their lives as if they were still living under the Old Covenant! This is especially sad when you consider that Christians have the Holy Spirit living inside their hearts and therefore have access to all the answers they could ever need. But because they have never developed a spiritual sensitivity or learned to recognize the voice of the Holy Spirit, they still live like Old Testament people, depending on special signs, divine signals, or advice from others.

This shouldn't be the case! *The Holy Spirit has come to tell you and me everything we need to know to walk in the fullness of God's plan for our lives.*

Because the Holy Spirit has come, the ignorance that once existed among God's people has permanently been *eliminated*. No one can rightfully use First Corinthians 2:9 as an excuse for ignorance or for not knowing the will of God. People who use this verse in this way are sadly misinformed about its purpose. Taken in context with the following verse, this verse clearly reveals that God does *not* want His people to be ignorant about His purposes, blessings, promises, and provisions that He has so meticulously planned for their lives.

First Corinthians 2:10 continues to tell us, "But God hath revealed them unto us by His Spirit...." What does the word "them" refer to? It refers to all the things that used to be hidden! The word "revealed" is the Greek word *apokalupsis*, a compound of the words *apo* and *kalupsis*. The word *apo* means *away*, and the word *kalupsis* is the Greek word for *a veil*, *a curtain*, or some type of *covering*.

When compounded into the word *apokalupsis*, which is normally translated as the word "revelation," it literally means *to remove the veil* or *to remove the curtain* so you can see what is on the other side.

This word *apokalupsis* plainly refers to *something that was veiled or hidden for a long time and suddenly becomes clear and visible to the mind or eye*. It is like pulling the curtains out of the way so you can see the scene outside your window. The view was always there for you to enjoy, but the curtains blocked your ability to see the real picture. Once the curtains are drawn apart, you suddenly behold what was previously hidden from your view. The moment you see beyond the curtain for the first time and observe what has been there all along but wasn't evident to you — *that* is what the Bible calls a "revelation."

Now apply this to First Corinthians 2:9,10. In verse 9, Paul indeed said that there was a time in the past when the eye could not see, the ear could not hear, nor could the heart begin to imagine all the amazing, wonderful things God had prepared for those who love Him. God had prepared those benefits according to His prearranged plan, but they were veiled — *hidden* to us, obscured from our sight. But when Jesus ascended, the Holy Spirit came, and one of His major works in our lives is to remove the veil that once obstructed our view so our eyes can see, our ears can hear, and our hearts can fully comprehend the specific, special plans that God has meticulously prepared for each of us!

So I want to tell you, if you've been using this verse to claim ignorance of God's ways, it's time for you to change your thinking and speaking about it! This verse doesn't give us an excuse for ignorance. In fact, it says just the opposite! This verse declares *the day of not knowing what God has prepared for us is gone forever*! The Holy Spirit — the *Great Revealer* — now lives inside our hearts, and He wants to reveal God's blessings, promises, provisions, and plans to you and to me!

Thank God, you no longer have to seek special signs or divine signals. You don't have to seek out prophets as they did in the Old Testament. Right inside your heart is the greatest Source of revelation on planet earth — the Holy Spirit! *If you'll develop a spiritual sensitivity and learn to listen to His voice, He will reveal everything that God has meticulously planned for you so you can be all God has destined you to be.*

My Prayer for Today

Lord, I thank You for the presence and the ministry of the Holy Spirit in my life. Forgive me for the times I've ignored this precious Partner whom You have sent to instruct and lead me in all the affairs of life. I repent for trying to find my way in life without His counsel and assistance. I confess that I've often sought the advice of family, friends, counselors, pastors, books, and other sources more than I've sought the counsel of the Holy Spirit — yet He is the One who knows the end from the beginning. Father, I thank You for providing the greatest source of revelation inside my own heart through His presence within me. Starting today, I seek the guidance of the Holy Spirit for each and every decision I make in life. Father, since You have meticulously planned my life and have sent the Holy Spirit to reveal that plan to me, from this day onward I want to let the Holy Spirit provide the revelation I need to fulfill that plan! I pray this in Jesus' name!

My Confession for Today

I declare that I am led by the Holy Spirit and that He reveals to me the will of God for my life. I am not ignorant, and I am not left to find my way on my own. God loves me so much that He sent the Holy Spirit to dwell within me and to provide me with all the details of God's awesome plan for my life. As I develop my spiritual sensitivity and listen to the Holy Spirit's voice, I am enlightened step by step to what He wants me to do with every part of my life. Because the Holy Spirit dwells in me, my eyes see, my ears hear, and my heart is able to comprehend the things God has planned for me! I declare this by faith in Jesus' name!

Questions for You to Consider

1. Do you know the overall framework of God's plan for your life? If so, what is it? Could you clearly state God's will and plan for your life if someone asked you to do it?

    _____

    _____

    _____

    _____

    _____

    _____

2. Are you spiritually developing so you can more and more easily perceive the voice of the Holy Spirit in your heart? What steps can you start taking to increase your level of spiritual sensitivity?

    _____

    _____

    _____

    _____

    _____

    _____

3. If someone were to ask you for help in determining God's will for his life, what would you tell him to do?

    _____

    _____

    _____

    _____

    _____

    _____

Day 2

The Prophetic Ministry of the Holy Spirit

> *Howbeit, when he, the Spirit of truth is come, he will guide you into all truth: for he shall not speak of himself; but whatsoever he shall hear, that shall he speak: and he will shew you things to come.*
>
> — John 16:13

There is no second-guessing when it comes to the leadership of the Holy Spirit. That's what Jesus stressed as He continued teaching His disciples about the ministry of the Holy Spirit. In John 16:13, Jesus said, "Howbeit, when he, the Spirit of Truth is come, he will guide you into all truth: for He shall not speak of Himself; but whatsoever He shall hear, that shall He speak: and He will *shew* you things to come."

The word "shew" in this verse is the Greek word *anagello*, which means *to announce* and describes *a vivid showing* or *a pronouncing of events*. So we see that part of the ministry of the Holy Spirit is *to announce* future events to us — and to show them to us with great clarity. The Holy Spirit does *not* portray a blurry picture of the future. If we listen to Him, He will vividly show us things to come so we can plan our lives according to His will.

This aspect of the Holy Spirit's ministry is evident in nearly every book of the Bible. For example, when the apostle Paul described the events that will occur in society at the end of the age (*see* 2 Timothy 3), he was writing under the prophetic ministry of the Holy Spirit. Likewise, the Holy Spirit is the One who imparted the vivid details to the apostle John concerning end-time events recorded in the book of Revelation.

However, this "revealing" ministry of the Holy Spirit is not relegated to Scripture. Jesus was speaking to *every* believer when He spoke of the Holy Spirit showing us things to come. If what Jesus taught is true — *and it is* — a significant part of the Holy Spirit's ministry is to reveal details about future events. He wants to prophetically speak to you and prepare you for your future. He wants to show you details about your future and the future of your family that He believes you need to know.

Open your heart today to the revealing work of the Holy Spirit. If anyone wants you to be prepared, it is the Holy Spirit, your Helper and Coach. He does not want you to be taken off guard by *any* situation you might encounter in life.

Simply avail yourself to Him by spending time in prayer every day without distraction. Linger in God's presence long enough to get your mind quiet and your heart open to hear. Then ask Him, "Holy Spirit, show me things to come in my life, in my business, and in my family. Reveal to me what I need to know to navigate every future situation that I will face with Your wisdom. I purpose to follow Your leading every step of the way."

My Prayer for Today

Holy Spirit, today I receive You as One who speaks into my life to show me things to come that I really need to know. I've tried hard to figure out things on my own. Forgive me for not developing my trust in You the way I should have in this area of my life. Starting right now, I ask You to fulfill the prophetic role of Your ministry in my life and to show me things to come. I know You want me to know how to plan my life, how to circumvent demonic attacks, and how to be prepared for every phase of my journey in You. Your Word promises that as I keep my spiritual ear tuned to You, You will show me exactly what I need to know about every step in front of me. I believe You and I gratefully receive Your ministry in my life day by day. I pray this in Jesus' name!

My Confession for Today

I confess that my ears are open and that my spirit is attuned to the voice of the Holy Spirit. Jesus said that He would show me things to come, and by faith, I embrace the prophetic ministry of the Holy Spirit in my life to show me everything I need to know about my future. I am not left to figure anything out on my own. The Holy Spirit speaks to my heart about things to come. I listen to His directions, and I make plans to do what He shows me. This spares me wasted time, helps me avoid mistakes, and puts me on a solid path that leads to His highest will for my life. I declare this by faith in Jesus' name!

Questions for You to Consider

1. One of the Holy Spirit's roles is to show you things to come. Have you learned to let the Holy Spirit speak prophetically to you about your future, or have you just tried to figure it all out on your own?

_____

_____

_____

_____

_____

2. Can you think of a time when the Holy Spirit _did_ tell you something about your future and you believed Him — and as a result, it gave you direction and saved you lots of valuable time and effort?

_____

_____

_____

_____

_____

3. Can you think of a time when the Holy Spirit clearly spoke to you, impressing your spirit with vital information, and you discounted and ignored it — only to understand later that it really was the Holy Spirit trying to show you something about your future that you really needed to know?

_____

_____

_____

_____

_____

_____

Day 3

Jesus and the Holy Spirit

> *He that believeth on me, as the scripture hath said, out of his belly shall flow rivers of living water. (But this spake he [Jesus] of the Spirit, which they that believe on him should receive: for the Holy Ghost was not yet given; because that Jesus was not yet glorified.)*
>
> — John 7:38,39

If anyone ever understood the ministry of the Holy Spirit, it was the Lord Jesus Christ. Jesus' earthly ministry was completely dependent upon the Holy Spirit. From His birth, nothing that happened to Him and nothing He did was apart from the power of the Holy Spirit. Moreover, when He sat down at the Father's right hand in Heaven, the first thing He did was send the Holy Spirit upon the Church on the day of Pentecost.

The ministry of Jesus and the ministry of the Holy Spirit are inseparable. In fact, when Jesus spoke of the Holy Spirit's future ministry to His Church in John 7:38 and 39, He was describing the Holy Spirit's present ministry through *Him* during His earthly ministry: "...Out of his belly shall flow rivers of living water. (But this spake he [Jesus] of the Spirit)...." The Greek word translated "flow" is a form of the word *rheo*, which pictures a rushing stream, so full that it actually overflows its banks.

This is how Jesus described His own relationship with the Holy Spirit as He walked this earth — and how He foretold the nature of the relationship that those who believed on Him would one day experience with the Holy Spirit after Jesus' death and resurrection. Jesus depended on the continual flow of the Holy Spirit's power, wisdom, counsel, and ability through Him and upon Him during His earthly ministry. And as He is, so are we to be in this world (1 John 4:17).

So let's take it further and consider these important facts about the workings of the Holy Spirit in the life and ministry of Jesus on this earth:

- Jesus was conceived by the Holy Spirit in the womb of the virgin Mary (*see* Matthew 1:18-20; Luke 1:35).

- Jesus' conception in Mary's womb was confirmed by Elisabeth, Mary's cousin, when she was filled with the Holy Spirit (*see* Luke 1:41-45).

- Jesus' dedication as a baby in the temple was accompanied by the supernatural manifestation of the Holy Spirit as Simeon, the priest, and Anna, the prophetess, prophesied over Him (*see* Luke 2:25-38).

- Jesus' public ministry was announced by John the Baptist, who, under the anointing of the Holy Spirit, declared that Jesus was the One who would baptize in the Holy Spirit and with fire (*see* Matthew 3:11; Luke 3:16; John 1:33; Acts 11:16).

- Jesus spoke of the baptism in the Holy Spirit and commanded the disciples to stay in Jerusalem until they had received this special endowment of power (*see* Luke 24:49; Acts 1:4,5).

- Jesus was empowered by the Holy Spirit at the Jordan River when He was baptized by John the Baptist (*see* Matthew 3:16; Mark 1:10; Luke 3:22; John 1:32).

- Jesus was given the fullness of the Spirit without measure (*see* John 3:34).

- Jesus was led by the Holy Spirit (*see* Matthew 4:1; Mark 1:12; Luke 4:1).

- Jesus returned from the wilderness in the power of the Holy Spirit (*see* Luke 4:14).

- Jesus stated publicly that His ministry was a result of the power of the Holy Spirit (*see* Luke 4:18).

- Jesus proclaimed that we must be born again by the Holy Spirit (*see* John 3:5-8).

- Jesus warned about the danger of blaspheming the Holy Spirit (*see* Matthew 12:31,32; Mark 3:28,29; Luke 12:10).

- Jesus taught about the work and ministry of the Holy Spirit (*see* Matthew 10:20; Mark 13:11; Luke 11:13; Luke 12:12; John 7:39; John 14:16,17; John 15:26; John 16:7-15).

- Jesus offered Himself upon the Cross, like a Lamb without spot or blemish, through the power of the Holy Spirit (*see* Hebrews 9:14).

- Jesus breathed the Holy Spirit into the disciples after His resurrection (*see* John 20:22).

- Jesus, once exalted to the right hand of the Father, poured out the Holy Spirit upon the Church on the day of Pentecost (*see* Acts 2:2-4, 2:33).

- Jesus instructed the disciples through the ministry of the Holy Spirit (*see* Acts 1:2).

Jesus and the Holy Spirit were always together when He was on the earth. If Jesus needed this kind of ongoing partnership with the Holy Spirit in order to accomplish His divine role in the earth, *you* must have that same partnership with the Spirit of God to fulfill what God has asked you to do. The Holy Spirit has been sent by Jesus to give you everything you need to be a victorious, successful, faith-filled, overcoming child of God in this world. With Him at your side, you are equipped for every situation you could ever face in life.

Because no one has ever known the Holy Spirit better than Jesus, we must look to see what Jesus had to say about His personality, His power, His gifts, and His character. In John 14, 15, and 16, the Lord Jesus Christ gives us important instruction about how to develop our own partnership with the Holy Spirit.

My Prayer for Today

Father, my heart yearns to know the Person of the Holy Spirit more deeply and to experience His power personally. I ask You to reveal truths and grant me understanding so I can cooperate with and respond to the Holy Spirit's ministry in my life. Father, I desire to walk in the spiritual depth and fullness that Jesus made available to me when He prayed in John 14 that You would send the Helper, the Holy Spirit, to indwell me. I ask You to open the door for me to embark on a spiritual path that I've never been on before. I know that this is Your will for me, so today I come before Your throne boldly and confidently to receive this with gratitude and joy! I pray this prayer in Jesus' name!

My Confession for Today

I confess that it is God's will for me to know the Person, power, and work of the Holy Spirit. In John 14, 15, and 16, Jesus taught explicitly about the Holy Spirit so that every believer could learn about the Spirit of God and knowledgeably respond to and experience His power. I recognize that this is why Jesus taught so much about the Holy Spirit's ministry in those three chapters. Therefore, I boldly declare that I will act on the truths I learn in the days to come about the Holy Spirit and His work in my life. I choose to cooperate with God as I embark on a new, deeper, and higher walk with God's Spirit than I've ever known before in my life. I declare this by faith in Jesus' name!

Questions for You to Consider

1. Can you describe what you know about the Person, power, and work of the Holy Spirit? Honestly, how well do you understand the work of the Holy Spirit?

   _____

   _____

   _____

   _____

   _____

   _____

2. When you approach this subject, what feelings do you have? Excitement and anticipation — or bewilderment, intimidation, and fear?

   _____

   _____

   _____

   _____

   _____

3. Does your church allow the Holy Spirit to move in its church services? In what ways does the Holy Spirit operate there? Are gifts of the Holy Spirit in open manifestation in your church? What are these gifts?

_____

_____

_____

_____

_____

_____

Day 4

The Holy Spirit Is Our Seal and Guarantee

> *In whom ye also trusted, after that ye heard the word of truth, the gospel of your salvation: in whom also after that ye believed, ye were sealed with that Holy Spirit of promise.*
>
> — **Ephesians 1:13**

In Greek and Roman times — and in certain places still today — if a package was to be dispatched to another location, it *first* went through a series of investigations to make sure the contents were not flawed, broken, or shattered. The sender would examine every single piece of the contents to make sure each one was whole and intact. This means the process of examining every little fragment of the contents was extraordinarily important for the one charged with *sealing* the shipment. If everything was whole and intact, the sender would pour hot wax on the crease of the package and then carefully push the insignia of the owner into the wax, signifying that all the contents were in perfect order. That "seal" was called a *sphragidzo* — the exact same word used in Ephesians 1:13, where the Bible says we were "sealed" with the Holy Spirit on the day we believed in the Lord Jesus Christ.

This insignia on the package was important for several reasons. It was the *insignia of the owner* of the package. No one would dare break into the sealed package to disturb the contents, especially if this owner was a high-ranking person, for the consequences of such an action would be severe.

Furthermore, that insignia, or "seal," was *the guarantee that the package would be delivered to its final destination.* It was like the highest postage stamp one could put on a package. The seal guaranteed that it would arrive at its ultimate destination unharmed.

Last but not least, that insignia *guaranteed that everything in the package was in order* — nothing was missing, broken, inferior, or shattered. Everything was whole and complete.

As I've noted, this Greek word *sphragidzo* ("seal") is precisely the word used in Ephesians 1:13, where Paul wrote, "...In whom also after that ye believed, ye were *sealed* with that Holy Spirit of promise."

This tells us that when we believed and were born again, God examined us to make sure we were made completely new and whole, and He found no flaws, no defects, and no shattered places. God saw that we were truly a product of Christ's own making and were complete in Him. In fact, we were *so* complete that, figuratively speaking, Christ poured His "wax" onto our hearts and spirits and then pressed the insignia of the Holy Spirit into us, giving guaranteed proof through the Spirit's indwelling presence that we belong to God and will make it to our ultimate destination — *Heaven.*

You and I may feel that we've had a few bumps along the way, but the Holy Spirit is the *guaranteed proof* that we will eventually make it to our heavenly home! Regardless of how the devil or life may try to assail against us, the Holy Spirit is "postage-paid sufficient" to get us all the way to our Lord Jesus one of these glorious days!

My Prayer for Today

Father, I thank You for sending someone to preach the Gospel to me — and for giving me the faith to believe it. I am in wonder and amazement that as soon as I believed, You gave me the Holy Spirit. The Spirit's presence in me is absolute, guaranteed proof that I belong to You — and I am so thankful that You pressed the insignia of the Holy Spirit into my heart and spirit, which means "postage-paid." Because of this precious work You've done in my life, I rejoice that one day I will reach my destination to be with You in my heavenly home! I pray this in Jesus' name!

My Confession for Today

I confess that I am complete and whole in Jesus Christ. After I believed, God saw that I was truly a product of Christ's own making. God made a full examination of me to make sure all parts were complete and that I was whole in Jesus Christ. Then He gave me the gift of the Holy Spirit, who will be with me all my life as a guarantee. He is the proof that I am a child of God. He is the evidence that I am born again. And His presence in my life is the guarantee that I will make it one day to my heavenly home! I declare this by faith in Jesus' name!

Questions for You to Consider

1. According to the Bible, you received the Holy Spirit the day you surrendered your life to Jesus Christ. Can you recall the change that occurred inside you when God made you His temple and sent His Spirit to dwell within you? What were some of the immediate changes you experienced?

_____

_____

_____

_____

_____

_____

2. When you read that God checked you out — that He investigated you to make sure you were really born again and whole — and found that you *were*, what does that mean to you? Think of it: *God found no defects!*

_____

_____

_____

_____

_____

3. If you've ever wondered if you will actually make it to Heaven, you can put that thought away forever *if* you have the Holy Spirit living inside you. He is the "postage paid," absolute guarantee that you will make it to your heavenly home. When you think about that, how does it make you feel?

_____

_____

_____

_____

_____

_____

Day 5

The Holy Spirit Earnestly Yearns for You!

> *Do ye think that the scripture saith in vain, the spirit that dwelleth in us lusteth to envy?*
>
> — James 4:5

Has there ever been anything you wanted so badly that you just couldn't get it off your mind? Every time you tried to think about something else, your mind just kept drifting back over and over again to that thing you desired. Finally, your urge to possess it became so intense that every fiber of your being wanted to reach out and capture it before anyone else had a chance to snatch it first!

Let me use a different illustration to make this point. If a drug addict or an alcoholic abruptly decides to stop doing drugs or drinking after many years of chemical abuse, what happens? Unless that person has a miraculous deliverance, it probably won't be too long before his body begins to crave those chemicals. In fact, his appetite for drugs or alcohol might get so forceful that he doubles over in agony. That's how much his body yearns for a "fix" of what it has habitually received in the past.

In the New Testament, the images above would be depicted by the Greek word *epipotheo,* which is a compound of the words *epi* and *potheo.* The word *epi* means *over*, and the word *potheo* is the word for *desire.* But when these two words are compounded together, the new word *epipotheo* portrays *an intense desire, a craving, a hunger, an ache, a yearning for something, a longing or pining for something.* More specifically, it describes *an intense, abnormal, excessive yearning.*

Usually this word is used to indicate an intense yearning for something that is morally wrong and sinful. It is the pitiful picture of someone, such as a drug addict or an alcoholic, who needs his "fix" so seriously that he is doubled over, racked with pain, and crying out, *"Please, someone, give me what I need!"*

Remarkably, this Greek word *epipotheo* is the same word found in James 4:5 to describe the desire of the Holy Spirit when it says, "...The spirit that dwelleth in us *lusteth* to envy...."

The word "lust" in this verse is from this same Greek word *epipotheo.* Only this time the word is not used to describe the painful addiction of a drug addict or alcoholic; rather, it depicts the Spirit of God! There is obviously some object that the Spirit of God craves. In fact, this Greek word pictures Him as desiring it so desperately that He is like one who needs some type of "fix" to satisfy an addiction. He is crying out, "I have to have it! I can't wait any longer! Give me what I crave! Give me what I am aching and yearning to have!"

But what does this mean? What is James 4:5 saying to us? What does the Holy Spirit yearn for so sincerely that the Bible would picture Him in this way?

In James 4:5, the Bible reveals the intense yearning the Holy Spirit possesses to have *us* entirely for Himself. That should be no surprise to us. He is our Indweller, our Sealer, our Sanctifier, and our Source of power. His attention, His gifts, His power, and His Word are all directed toward us. He is in love with us!

The Holy Spirit is so in love with us that He wants more, more, more, and more of us. Every day He wants our time, our attention, our devotion, and our fellowship. If we deny the Holy Spirit of what He wants from us, He cries out, "I need you! I must have you! I want to fill you, empower you, and flood you with My divine life!"

James 4:5 conveys this compelling idea:

> *"...The Spirit has an all-consuming and passionate desire to have more and more of us. In fact, this desire to possess us is so strong that He literally yearns, craves, and pines after us."*

Never forget that the Holy Spirit is a Divine Lover who lives on the inside of us. He passionately yearns to fulfill His responsibility to the Father to help, teach, guide, and empower us. The word *epipotheo* emphatically means that when it comes to you and me, the Holy Spirit can never get enough!

The Holy Spirit desires to possess you — *all of you*. Because of this intense desire, He is focused on changing you, empowering you, conforming you to the image of Jesus Christ, and helping you fulfill God's plan for your life.

Learn how to yield to the Holy Spirit. Allow Him to have more and more of you each day. *Satisfy the yearning of this Divine Lover. Let the Holy Spirit love you! Let Him control you! Let Him exercise His authority in your life and flood you with His divine desire!*

My Prayer for Today

Lord, help me to be mindful that the Holy Spirit lives inside me and wants to possess more and more of me every day. Please help me learn how to surrender to the Spirit's power and to yield to His sanctifying presence. I know that as I yield to Him, He will fill me full of every good thing I need to live a happy and successful life in this world. I want to begin today by opening myself to the Holy Spirit completely. Holy Spirit, I ask You to fill me anew right now. I pray this in Jesus' name!

My Confession for Today

I confess that the Holy Spirit loves me! He thinks of me, dreams of me, and wants to fill me with His presence and power. The Holy Spirit was sent into this world to be my Helper, my Guide, my Teacher, and my Leader. Therefore, I am learning to lean on Him and to let Him lead me through all my affairs in this life. I surrender to Him, yield to Him, and depend on Him for everything I need. I declare this by faith in Jesus' name!

Questions for You to Consider

1. Have you ever experienced the deep love that the Holy Spirit has for you?

    _____

    _____

    _____

    _____

    _____

    _____

2. When you had this experience, where were you and what was happening in your life?

    _____

    _____

    _____

    _____

    _____

    _____

3. In order for you to continually experience the deep love of the Holy Spirit, what do you need to do?

_____

_____

_____

_____

_____

_____

Day 6

You Are a Shrine for the Holy Spirit

> *What? know ye not that your body is the temple of the Holy Ghost which is in you, which ye have of God, and ye are not your own? For ye are bought with a price: therefore glorify God in your body, and in your spirit, which are God's.*
>
> — **1 Corinthians 6:19,20**

Russia is a nation with more than one thousand years of Russian Orthodox religious history. One of the greatest signs of this religious history is located right in the heart of Moscow — a gigantic white marble cathedral with golden domes that is called "Christ the Savior." I've traveled the world and seen a lot in my life, but when it comes to decorative architecture, this building is by far one of the most splendid I've ever seen. Its interior is highly adorned with ornamentations of gold, silver, and precious stones. It is embellished like no other building I've ever seen anywhere else.

When we hear the word "shrine," this is normally the type of image that passes through our minds. We see arched and vaulted ceilings, marble, granite, gold, silver, hand-carved etchings, and lots and lots of smoke from incense being burned as a part of worship. Shrines are not comfortable places where we'd want to live, but their ornamentation is certainly impressive. A shrine is a beautiful place to visit, but we wouldn't want to live there!

The Greek word *naos* is the word for *a temple* or *a highly decorated shrine*, like the one illustrated in the story above. This Greek word is the very word the apostle Paul used when he told the Corinthians, "...Know ye not that your body is the temple of the Holy Ghost which is in you...?" (1 Corinthians 6:19).

Because the Corinthians were Greek and had grown up in a classical Greek culture, they had seen temples their entire lives. So when Paul used this word *naos*, it would have been natural for images like the ones above to flash through their minds. They knew that the word *naos* always depicted *a highly decorated shrine*. The temples of their times were beautiful buildings with tall, vaulted ceilings, marble columns, granite floors, hand-carved woodwork overlaid with gold and silver, and burning incense billowing into the air around the front of the altar.

Shrines like the one I described above are imposing and impressive; however, they're *not* comfortable. But when the Holy Spirit came into your heart, He made a home that was so comfortable, He was actually happy to come live inside you! He moved in, settled down, and permanently took up residency in your heart — *His new home*!

You see, when you got saved, the ultimate miracle was performed inside your heart. The Holy Spirit took your spirit, which had been dead in trespasses and sin, and raised it to new life. His work inside you was so glorious that when it was all finished, He declared you to be His own workmanship (Ephesians 2:10). At that moment, your spirit became *a marvelous temple of God!*

What does all this mean?

- 🔥 When we were born again, we were inwardly created to become a dwelling place of God.

- 🔥 Our bodies are not mere shacks or mud huts; rather, we are inwardly fashioned to be magnificent dwelling places for the Spirit of God.

- 🔥 Because the fruit of the Spirit, the gifts of the Spirit, and the grace of God are working inside us, we are inwardly embellished with rich spiritual ornamentation.

- 🔥 Our inner man is now a temple that is so marvelous, no human eye has ever seen anything like it!

If you've been dealing with a poor self-image, grab hold of this truth, because this is the greatest self-image booster that exists! Inwardly you are so beautiful and magnificent that Almighty God wanted to live inside you! What kind of home do you think God would require? A shabby shack made of dirt and sticks? No! He has built for Himself a beautiful temple within your heart — and that is who you are right now! *Now live like the magnificently decorated cathedral of God's Spirit that you are!*

My Prayer for Today

Lord, I am so excited to think that You made my heart Your home. It is so overwhelming to think that You want to live inside me. Help me see myself as Your dwelling place and to honor Your presence inside me by the kind of life I lead. I want to bless You and honor You, so please help me do the right things that bring You the greatest pleasure and joy. I pray this in Jesus' name!

My Confession for Today

I gratefully acknowledge that my body is the temple of the Holy Spirit. Yes, the Holy Spirit lives inside me. My heart is not a hotel where He occasionally visits; rather, my heart has become His home. He has invested His power, His gifts, His fruit, and the life of Jesus Christ in me. Inwardly I am highly adorned with the goodness of God. My spirit is so marvelously created in Christ Jesus that God Himself is comfortable to live inside me! I declare this by faith in Jesus' name!

Questions for You to Consider

1. Are you living like the magnificently decorated cathedral of God's Spirit that you are?

   _____

   _____

   _____

   _____

   _____

   _____

2. How can you make use of the rich ornamentation you have on the inside of you: the fruit of the Spirit, the gifts of the Spirit, and the grace of God?

   _____

   _____

   _____

   _____

   _____

   _____

3. How would you behave differently if you truly believed that the Holy Spirit has permanently moved into your life and redecorated the place?

_____

_____

_____

_____

_____

_____

Day 7

The Guiding Ministry of the Holy Spirit

> *Howbeit, when he, the Spirit of truth is come, he will guide you into all truth....*
>
> — John 16:13

In most Middle Eastern countries, ancient ruins are scattered throughout the land, dating from biblical times. To visit these sites, it is required that a person be accompanied by an "official guide." These guides are certified by the government and undergo a rigorous certification, which must be renewed annually. The process requires guides to receive ongoing education and training in a variety of subjects, such as history, art, and archeology, in addition to earning their initial degrees. Official guides are not simply individuals who snapped a "tour guide" badge on their shirt or jacket; they are highly trained specialists who invested years of study in order to obtain and maintain that hard-earned status.

To make a tour interesting for a group, a guide must know how to communicate effectively and give clear instructions concerning where to go, what to stay away from, and so on. Hiring good guides can be expensive because they have spent so many years studying and training. However, their expertise is invaluable. As they lead people through a site, tour guides impart information that can be obtained only through many years of studying — a commitment that most people obviously cannot make.

In many large, complex sites, such as the ancient ruins of Ephesus and Pergamum in modern-day Turkey, it would almost be foolish to try to see these sites without a certified guide. These sites are huge, and parts of the ancient roads are deteriorated, twisted, rocky, and potentially dangerous. In fact, there are so many paths to take that an uninformed person could easily get confused and lost along the way. However, with a good guide at your side, you can rest assured that you will not get hurt or lost as you explore, and you'll conclude your experience with a wonderful memory of a trip well executed.

With this example in mind, let's look at John 16:13, where Jesus told His disciples, "Howbeit, when he, the Spirit of truth is come, he will guide you into all truth...." In this verse, Jesus used the example of a tour guide to describe the guiding ministry of the Holy Spirit in our lives. Just as a guide leads a group through a historical site, the Holy Spirit wants to guide us through life.

The word "guide" in John 16:13 is the Greek word *odega* — a word that describes a *tour guide* or *one who would lead you on an excursion.* As we have seen, a tour guide is a professional who has gained an intimate knowledge of a site you want to see through years of dedication and experience. He knows all the shortcuts and all the points of interest, and he can relate its history in depth. Your willingness to allow the guide to lead and your willingness to follow his directions will save you from making mistakes and drawing incorrect conclusions about where you are, where you are headed, and what are you are seeing.

This Greek word *odega* describes the guiding ministry of the Holy Spirit in our lives. Jesus was informing us that if we are willing to listen to the Holy Spirit and to follow His instructions, He will act as a Guide for our lives. Like the tour guides discussed in the example above, the Holy Spirit knows what lies ahead of us. He knows the obstacles we should avoid; He sees our ultimate destination; and He knows God's plan for our lives down to the smallest detail. The Holy Spirit knows every route God desires for us to take — and if we are willing to follow the Spirit's leading, He will give us a wonderful and memorable experience along the path of life.

My friend, I want to tell you that the Holy Spirit deeply desires to guide you in life. If you'll let Him lead you, He will offer you sound guidance in every sphere of your life. If you listen to His voice, He will tell you the career you should choose, the person you should marry, and the place you should live. He is the only One who knows the future; therefore, He is the only One who is truly qualified to lead and guide you.

Divine guidance is one of the biggest challenges we face in the Christian life. However, Jesus explicitly said that the Holy Spirit is here to lead and guide us every step along the way. What a relief and security it affords us to know that God the Father has charged the Holy Spirit with the responsibility of leading and guiding us to the right place at the right time — every single time. And He also warns us *away from* certain people, places, and situations. This is His job! Without His direction, we are incapable of discerning where we should go in life, the people with whom we should surround ourselves, and the best timing for our endeavors.

However, in order for this to happen, we have to make an effort to listen to the Holy Spirit's voice and be willing to follow His instruction. If we will do that, we'll find that the Spirit of God is leading us, just as He did the apostles in the book of Acts!

Today I urge you to open your heart to the guiding ministry of the Holy Spirit. Trust that He is the Spirit of Truth who will not mislead you. "Take the hand" of the Holy Spirit and tell Him from your heart: "Holy Spirit, I trust You from this moment forward to be my Guide every step of the way!"

My Prayer for Today

Holy Spirit, I open my heart to Your leading and guiding in life. I repent for foolishly having tried to lead myself through difficult decisions and questions, when you were always right there, wanting to lead me along the way. You know the plan of God for me down to the smallest detail, and from this time forward, I will do my best to consult You and to yield to Your guidance for my life. You know everything about me, my future, and which steps I need to take next. Rather than try to figure it all out on my own, I entrust myself to you as my official Guide to lead me each step of the way! I pray this in Jesus' name!

My Confession for Today

I declare by faith that I am led by the Holy Spirit. He was sent to lead and direct me, and I am learning to hear His voice, to recognize His leading, and to allow Him to be the Senior Guide in my life. I know that as a result of being guided by the Spirit, my life is going to be more adventuresome and filled with less mistakes, for the Holy Spirit is the Spirit of Truth, and He will never lead me down a wrong path. Holy Spirit, I'm ready — let's get started today! I declare this by faith in Jesus' name!

Questions for You to Consider

1. Can you think of a moment in your life when the Holy Spirit supernaturally led you through difficult decisions and questions? When was that experience, and have you ever shared it with anyone else?

_____

_____

_____

_____

_____

2. How do you recognize the guidance of the Holy Spirit? If someone asked you to describe what it is like to be led by the Holy Spirit, how would you put it into words? Why don't you practice describing it so you'll be ready to help someone else understand what it is like to receive guidance from the Holy Spirit?

_____

_____

_____

_____

_____

3. What situation are you facing right now that requires supernatural direction? How will you let the Holy Spirit guide you down the path that lies before you?

_____

_____

_____

_____

_____

_____

Day 8

Don't Put Out the Spirit's Fire!

> *Quench not the Spirit.*
>
> — 1 Thessalonians 5:19

Have you ever sensed the Holy Spirit leading you to do something, but because of fear you were afraid to do it? Even though you were sure it was God's Spirit who was speaking to you, did you grit your teeth, dig in your heels, and decide that you would *not* do what He was leading you to do or say?

If the answer is *yes*, it's time for you to stop doing that! The Holy Spirit is trying to use you to help someone or to accomplish some feat according to His plans and purposes. Don't let the devil or a spirit of fear talk you out of experiencing the joy of being used by the Holy Spirit. This is exactly why Paul admonished us, "Quench not the Spirit" (1 Thessalonians 5:19).

The word "quench" in this verse is taken from the Greek word *sbennumi*. The word *sbennumi* means *to extinguish, smother, suppress, douse, put out, snuff out,* or *to quell.* It most often means *to extinguish a fire by dousing it with water.* In some places, it means *to evaporate* or *to dry up.*

There's no doubt about what Paul is trying to tell us. If we ignore the Holy Spirit's voice long enough and often enough, eventually we will become spiritually hardened and will no longer be able to hear Him when He does try to speak to us. It will be like His voice *evaporates* or *dries up*, and we will hear it no more.

You need to know that your own actions, fears, insecurities, and disobedience to the voice of the Holy Spirit can thwart the plan of God for your life! The Holy Spirit is willing and ready to give you a divine assignment, but you hinder His wonderful plans by ignoring and denying His right to use you time and time again.

If you've ever seen a campfire, you know that its flames can burn very bright and hot. But what happens if someone keeps throwing water on the coals? Initially it will only *dampen* the heat of the flames. But if the person continues to throw water on the flames, eventually that water will *quench, smother,* or *put out* the fire altogether.

Has the Holy Spirit been speaking to your heart, tenderly directing you to do something? Have you obeyed Him and done what He has prompted you to do — or have you turned a deaf ear to His voice? Let me encourage you:

> *Don't ignore the Holy Spirit's leading! Don't disregard His voice! Don't close your ears when He is speaking to you! Don't pass up an opportunity for the Holy Spirit to use you! Don't avoid moments when God wants to pour His power through you! Don't throw water on the flames until you quench the Spirit!*

Instead of continually shutting your ears to the Holy Spirit's voice and dousing the flames of the Spirit in your heart, it's time for you to say, "Yes, Lord, I'll do what You say. I'll go where You send me. I'll obey what You tell me to do!" When you adopt this attitude, you start putting fuel back on the fire again! Every time you say, "Yes, Lord," and follow through with obedience, you stoke the coals and cause the Holy Spirit's fire to burn more brightly in your life.

The primary reason we don't obey the prompting of the Holy Spirit is that we are afraid of what may or may not happen if we step out in faith to do what He has asked us to do. But we need to learn to trust the Holy Spirit. He will never lead us to do something that is wrong or harmful; He will never fail us or let us down.

Determine in your heart today to obey whatever the Spirit of God tells you to do. As you stay true to that decision, you'll see God do marvelous things through you. *He will use you to set people free from whatever holds them in bondage — all because you determined to do what the Holy Spirit led you to do!*

My Prayer for Today

Lord, help me to quickly obey when the Spirit of God prompts me to do something. The last thing I want to do is throw water on the flames of the Spirit in my heart. Forgive me for suffocating the life of the Holy Spirit in me by refusing to do what He tells me to do. From this point onward, I make the choice to quickly obey, but I need Your strength to do this. So today I am asking You to fill me anew with brand-new courage to step out in faith, to quickly obey, and to leave the results with You! I pray this in Jesus' name!

My Confession for Today

I confess that I am quick to obey the voice of the Holy Spirit. When He tugs at my heart, pointing me in a specific direction or leading me to minister to a certain person, I do not hold back, hesitate, or resist. Instead, I say, "Lord, I'll do whatever You want me to do!" I then step out in faith and watch as His power is demonstrated to me and through me! I declare this by faith in Jesus' name!

Questions for You to Consider

1. Can you think of a time when the Spirit of God prompted you to do something, but you dug in your heels and refused to do it?

_____

_____

_____

_____

_____

_____

2. How did you feel afterwards, knowing that you had resisted the voice of the Holy Spirit?

_____

_____

_____

_____

_____

3. How will you respond the next time the Holy Spirit tells you to do something?

_____

_____

_____

_____

_____

_____

Day 9

The Unseen Power Behind the Throne

> *...take ye no thought how or what thing ye shall answer, or what ye shall say: for the Holy Spirit shall teach you in the same hour what ye ought to say.*
>
> — Luke 12:11,12

In Moscow stands the Kremlin — an architectural wonder that is simply breathtaking in terms of beauty. Within this great walled city are palaces, ancient churches, governmental buildings, and the State Armory Museum, a fabulous structure that holds treasures, crowns, diamonds, carriages, and thrones of the Russian state. One throne in particular has captured my attention every time I visit the Armory. It is a gigantic, double-seated throne with a strange opening just behind the seat to the right side.

In 1676, Tsar Alexis Romanov died, leaving his sickly son, Ivan, to inherit the throne. As a result of a number of political manipulations, it was decided that

Ivan would be proclaimed tsar jointly with his ten-year-old brother, Peter. For a brief period of time, both brothers ruled Russia, sitting together on the gigantic, double-seated throne that is now on display in the Armory. Young Ivan sat on the left side of the throne, and his brother Peter sat on the seat to the right. Eventually Ivan proved to be too physically and mentally feeble to rule, so he resigned his position. His brother Peter remained as tsar and ruled Russia until his death in 1725. Today he is respectfully referred to as *Peter the Great* because of the great accomplishments and lasting impressions he made during his reign.

But why was there an opening behind the seat where Peter sat upon the throne? That opening was made so Peter's sister, Sophia, could sit behind the young tsar and privately provide him with correct responses to questions and comments made to him by visiting dignitaries. As the young tsar listened to his sister's words spoken quietly to him through a veil, and as he in turn communicated what he heard to those who approached him, an impression was made that he was intellectually powerful, even at an early age. The truth was, young Peter *was* brilliant, but his sister, although unseen, was the *real* power behind the throne.

When I've visited the State Armory Museum and looked at that strange opening in the double-seated throne, I've pondered the words of Jesus in Luke 12:11,12. Jesus told His disciples what to do when they faced difficult circumstances in which they didn't know what to say or how to respond: "…Take ye no thought how or what thing ye shall answer, or what ye shall say: for the Holy Spirit shall teach you in the same hour what ye ought to say."

Notice Jesus said, "…Take ye *no thought* how or what thing ye shall answer…." That doesn't mean Jesus was advocating mindlessness. Rather, He was saying that there is no need for us to be *anxious* or *worried* in those moments because the Holy Spirit will be the unseen presence, advising us what to say.

It would be easy in the natural for us to feel fretful, uneasy, upset, or distraught in those moments of not knowing how to answer. That's why it's important to understand that the Greek word for "thought" in this verse is actually Jesus' prohibition *against* our being fretful in such moments. We may not always know how to respond to every question put before us or every situation we face. But Jesus is telling us that we have no need to be ill at ease because His Spirit will teach us "in that hour" — that is, in our specific moment of need — *exactly* what we need to say.

The sister of Peter the Great was an invisible advisor to her brother as she sat behind the strange opening in that double-seated throne. But the Holy Spirit wants to be an infinitely more effective unseen Advisor to *you*. If you will allow Him to take that position in your life, and if you will determine to learn how to hear and trust His voice, the Holy Spirit will give you answers to the questions and situations you encounter that you're unable to answer or solve on your own.

So open your heart to the Holy Spirit today, and receive Him as your personal Advisor. As you train your heart to hear what He's saying to you more and more accurately, He will help you respond with His insight and wisdom to every situation you could ever face in this life!

My Prayer for Today

Father, I thank You for the wonderful ministry of the Holy Spirit. I repent for the times I've allowed myself to become fretful and upset because I didn't know what to do or say. Holy Spirit, I receive and give place to Your ministry as my personal, private, invisible Advisor. I allow You to take this position in my life, and I purpose in my heart to learn to hear and trust Your voice. Thank You for giving me answers to questions and situations that I would be unable to answer or to solve on my own. I pray this in Jesus' name!

My Confession for Today

I confess that the Holy Spirit is my personal Counselor. In every situation of life, I listen to the voice of the Spirit. He speaks to my heart and mind, and He tells me precisely what I am to say and what I am to do. I am not helpless, confused, or caught off guard because the Holy Spirit lives within me as my ever-present Helper. With Him inside me to guide me, I am never at a loss for wisdom in critical moments. He is my Helper, my Teacher, my Comforter, and my Advisor! I declare this by faith in Jesus' name!

Questions for You to Consider

1. Can you recall a moment when you had no answer for a question being put before you — and then suddenly the Holy Spirit showed you what to say and what to do? When was that experience? Is it something you could share with others to encourage them in similar moments?

   _____

   _____

   _____

   _____

   _____

   _____

2. What questions or situations are you facing right now that you do not naturally know how to answer or how to solve? Have you asked the Holy Spirit to help you?

   _____

   _____

   _____

   _____

   _____

   _____

Day 10

Jesus' Teaching in the Upper Room

> *I am not leaving you comfortless: I will come to you.*
>
> — **John 14:18**

I was raised in a wonderful church where we were doctrinally taught very well. But as I grew older, I began to become more and more spiritually hungry. It seemed there was a gaping hole inside my heart, and I yearned for more than what I knew about the Lord. That is when I began to learn of teaching about the ministry of the Holy Spirit that was different from anything I had ever been exposed to previously. Hearing those fresh teachings changed my life because they introduced me to the supernatural ministry of the Holy Spirit in a way I had never before experienced.

Starting today, I want to begin talking to you about those teachings on the Holy Spirit that so dramatically changed my life. To begin, let's go to the Upper Room where Jesus gathered His disciples on the eve of His crucifixion; where

He washed their feet; where He served them Communion; and where He took time to teach them about the ministry of the Holy Spirit.

On that last night when Jesus was in the Upper Room with His disciples, He knew that He was leaving the world and that these moments were actually His *last* opportunity to teach them. There was a myriad of subjects Jesus could have taught His disciples that night, but He knew that in His absence, they would need a powerful, ongoing relationship with the Holy Spirit. Consequently, Jesus devoted His last opportunity to teach them about the ministry of the Holy Spirit. In John chapters 14, 15, and 16, we find teachings by Jesus that are devoted primarily to the Person, power, and work of the Holy Spirit. We don't know the amount of time it took for Jesus to teach His disciples about the Holy Spirit during His last night on earth with them, but it's clear from these three chapters that He dedicated a significant amount of time.

That evening Jesus told the disciples that He would soon be departing the world. By reading John 14, it is clear that the disciples were tempted to despair when they heard this heavy news. They were tempted to feel abandoned, so Jesus told them, "I am not leaving you comfortless: I will come to you" (John 14:18).

Let's begin by looking at the word "comfortless" used in this verse. The word "comfortless" is a translation of the Greek word *orphanos*, and it is where we get the word *orphan*. A literal translation would be, "I will not leave you as orphans...." But in the time of the New Testament, this word had a wider range of meaning, for it was also used to describe students who felt abandoned by their teacher. However, whether this Greek word was used to describe orphans who had lost their parents or students who felt abandoned by a teacher, it always conveyed the idea of a person who felt deserted by someone whom they trusted and to whom they looked for guidance.

Jesus promised that although He was leaving this earth, He was not abandoning His disciples. He would come to them through the ministry of the

Holy Spirit, who would exactly represent Him to the disciples in every way. By sending the Holy Spirit, Jesus was sending a personal replacement to take His place among the disciples — One who would be with each of them all the time. This would be far better than when Jesus was on the earth and could only physically be in one place at a time. In fact, Jesus later said that the coming of the Holy Spirit would be far better for them (*see* John 16:7) because it would herald the unlimited presence of Christ in the earth. Through the work of the Holy Spirit, Christ could reside with every believer in every place on the earth simultaneously.

Once Jesus was exalted at the right hand of the Father, He took on the role of our Intercessor for all eternity (*see* Hebrews 7:25). Once seated, He poured out the gift of the Holy Spirit upon the Church (*see* Acts 2:33). Today the Holy Spirit is that Member of the Godhead who operates in the world. Christ is Lord *over* the Church, and the Holy Spirit carries out His Lordship *inside* the Church. We live in the age when the *Holy Spirit* operates in the world.

In Ephesians 1:13, the apostle Paul taught that the moment you receive your salvation, the Holy Spirit enters into you and serves as God's covenant seal on your life in Him. Therefore, if you have surrendered to the Lordship of Jesus Christ, the Holy Spirit has come to take up residency inside of you. Hear me clearly — the Holy Spirit *is* a Resident in the life of every person who has surrendered to the Lordship of Jesus Christ. In fact, Romans 8:9 says it is impossible to personally know God unless you have the Holy Spirit residing inside you. So rest assured, if you have come to that moment when you gave your life to Christ — that is, you surrendered to His Lordship — then the Holy Spirit has sealed you and has permanently moved into your heart. This means your heart is not just a hotel where He occasionally visits. *Your heart is His home.*

As glorious as it is that the Holy Spirit lives inside those who believe, this does not guarantee that they experience fellowship with Him. So today I'd like to ask you: What kind of *fellowship* do you have with the Holy Spirit? Is He a neglected Resident in your life, or do you actually experience regular, intimate fellowship with Him?

That night in the Upper Room, Jesus promised His disciples (and us) that when He ascended to Heaven, He would not abandon us like orphans or like students who had been deserted by their teacher. He promised that He would come to us through the ministry of the Holy Spirit, and Jesus kept His word! But just as any person must be recognized to be experienced, we must *on purpose* recognize the presence of the Holy Spirit if we are going to experience fellowship with Him in our lives.

If you have never stopped to recognize the Holy Spirit in your life or experienced what I call the fellowship of the Holy Spirit, today would be a wonderful time for you to begin! Just open your heart and say, "Holy Spirit, thank You for living inside me. Starting today I want to begin enjoying fellowship with You!"

My Prayer for Today

Holy Spirit, I want to begin enjoying fellowship with You. Since Jesus depended on You, I know that I need to depend on You too. So right now, more than ever before, I express my inner yearning to begin a new and deeper journey in learning how to have fellowship with You. I want to know You; I want to know Your power; and I ask You to come alongside and help me as Jesus said You would do! I pray this in Jesus' name!

My Confession for Today

I acknowledge that because I am a child of God, the Holy Spirit lives inside me as a continual Resident. He longs to have fellowship with me and to reveal the depths of Jesus' love to my heart. I repent for the times that I have ignored Him and treated Him as an unrecognized Resident. From this moment onward, I confess that I will live with an awareness of His presence and that I will embrace the wonderful ministry that He has come to provide for my life. I declare this by faith in Jesus' name!

Questions for You to Consider

1. Do you experience the fellowship of the Holy Spirit in your life? If yes, how would you describe the experience of fellowship with Him to someone else?

   _____

   _____

   _____

   _____

   _____

   _____

2. Can you recognize when the Holy Spirit is speaking to you? If yes, how would you describe the way you recognize His voice?

   _____

   _____

   _____

   _____

   _____

3. Have you had moments when the Holy Spirit led you in a super-natural way that dramatically affected your life? If yes, what were some of those moments, and what happened as a result?

_____

_____

_____

_____

_____

_____

Day 11

Jesus' Prayer

> *And I will pray the Father, and he shall give you another Comforter, that he may abide with you for ever.*
>
> — John 14:16

I can't begin to imagine how alarmed the disciples must have felt when Jesus told them that He would soon be leaving them. Jesus had often warned them that He would be leaving, but that evening in the Upper Room, as they spent their last hours together, the full weight of this reality began to dawn on the disciples — and it put them in a state of panic and dismay. John 14:2 tells us that Jesus was aware that their hearts were troubled.

It was natural for the disciples to feel sorrowful at the news of Jesus' imminent departure. Living and walking with Jesus was more than they had ever hoped for in this world. With Jesus at their side, their lives had been filled with adventure, excitement, joy, victory, power, healing, and miracles. What would life be like without Jesus? Would it ever be the same? Was this the end to their dreams?

Feelings of insecurity and uncertainty would have been normal for any human being in the disciples' position. They had grown dependent upon the physical, visible presence of Jesus — something we've never experienced and therefore cannot fully comprehend. But in the midst of the disciples' fears, Jesus promised them, "I will not leave you comfortless..." (John 14:18).

The word "comfortless" is from the Greek word *orphanos*, which is where we get the word *orphan*. As noted before, the word *orphanos* could describe children who had lost their parents, or it could describe students who were abandoned by their teacher. In both cases, it is the picture of younger, less educated, less knowledgeable people feeling deserted by those they trusted and looked to for guidance.

Jesus had become a spiritual Mentor to the disciples. For more than three years, these men had walked with Jesus and depended entirely upon Him. During those three years, Jesus' voice had been the only voice they had followed. They walked in His footsteps, and they explicitly followed His directions. As a Mentor, Jesus had taught them everything — how to cast out demons, how to heal the sick, how to travel in ministry, and on and on. The full extent of the spiritual training Jesus imparted to His disciples includes far too many truths to list here. In fact, Jesus had taught them *everything* they knew regarding spiritual matters.

But in John 14, Jesus made it clear that He would be leaving His disciples. Later that night, He was to be arrested in the Garden of Gethsemane, judged before the religious leaders of the city, sent to be judged by Pilate, then by Herod, and then back to Pilate again. And following these harrowing experiences, He was to be scourged, crucified, and buried. All of these events would occur in a mere matter of hours from those moments when Jesus sat with them in the

Upper Room and told them that He would be leaving. They simply had no idea how quickly He would be physically taken from them.

But Jesus knew. That is why it was so important for Him to take that last evening to teach the disciples about the ministry of the Holy Spirit. Jesus knew they would need to depend on the Holy Spirit as completely as *He* had depended on Him. So Jesus took His last hours to instruct them about the ministry of the Holy Spirit and introduce them to this spiritual Partner who would become their new Teacher and Guide in the world.

Jesus told the disciples in John 14:16, "I will *pray* the Father, and he shall give you another Comforter...." The word "pray" is the Greek word *eratao*, which was a legal word that described *a lawyer who would argue a case in a court of law*. It is interesting that this is the Greek word that was so crucial for the survival of the disciples that the Comforter would be sent that Jesus was going to the Father to present His case in that matter. This case would be so concrete — *so clear and unmistakable* — that the Father would respond to Jesus' request by sending the Comforter, *the Holy Spirit*, as His replacement to the disciples.

Imagine how important the ministry of the Holy Spirit must be for Jesus! Jesus was making the case clear to the Father that He *must* send the Holy Spirit, for the disciples — and then later the Church — would not survive without the Holy Spirit's help and assistance. The very fact that the word *eratao* is used to describe Jesus' petition to the Father tells us that the coming of the Holy Spirit was imperative. Jesus treated this request as one of the utmost importance. And if Jesus treated this subject so importantly, then we must treat it with equal importance.

So I encourage you to seriously ask yourself this question today: *How importantly do I treat the subject of the Holy Spirit in my life?* And whatever your answer, make it your priority in the days ahead to learn how to cooperate with the Holy Spirit's work in your life on a deeper level than you ever have before!

My Prayer for Today

Holy Spirit, I admit that I have often neglected to acknowledge Your presence in my life. I repent, and I ask You to please forgive me. It's not that I've tried to ignore You; I have just been ignorant of Your role in my life and how deeply I have needed Your fellowship. I confess that I've even had fears about opening my heart more deeply to You because of things I've seen and heard others do that seemed a little strange. Forgive me for being closed to You when, in fact, I cannot live the Christian life without Your power and Your help. Right now I take the next step to invite You to move powerfully in my life. I take down all the guards, and I decide to trust You to bring Jesus closer to me. I pray this in Jesus' name!

My Confession for Today

I declare that the Holy Spirit works mightily in my life. I am not afraid to surrender to the Holy Spirit's power. I acknowledge that I cannot successfully live the Christian life without His involvement, so I open every part of my life to Him and to His powerful workings. As a result, I am filled with spiritual power; I am supernaturally led by the Spirit of God because I am a child of God; and I am being transformed into the image of Jesus Christ. As a result of my fellowship and obedience to the Holy Spirit, my Christian life is filled with victory and adventure! I declare this by faith in Jesus' name!

Questions for You to Consider

1. Have you treated your relationship with the Holy Spirit as seriously as Jesus treated it? If not, why not?

    _____

    _____

    _____

    _____

    _____

    _____

2. Do you attend a church where your fellowship with the Holy Spirit will be encouraged or discouraged? If your church does not encourage you to go deeper with the Spirit of God, why are you still attending that church?

    _____

    _____

    _____

    _____

    _____

    _____

3. What concrete steps can you take to start developing a deeper fellowship with the Holy Spirit? For example, you could read books on the Holy Spirit that will take you deeper in your spiritual walk, or you could listen to teachings on the subject of the Holy Spirit. What other things can you think of to do to enhance your fellowship with the Holy Spirit?

_____

_____

_____

_____

_____

_____

Day 12

The Comforter, Part 1

> *And I will pray the Father, and he shall give you another Comforter....*
>
> **— John 14:16**

As Jesus taught His disciples about the Holy Spirit during their last night together in the Upper Room, He referred to the Holy Spirit as the "Comforter" on four separate occasions (*see* John 14:16, 14:26, 15:26, and John 16:7). For Jesus to repeat this title *four times* in the space of three chapters tells us that the point He is making must be very important. When a truth is repeated in quick succession in Scripture, it is always for the sake of emphasis. Here we find that Jesus was trying to penetrate His disciples' hearts — *as well as our own hearts* — with the truth of the Holy Spirit's role as a "Comforter" so they would fully understand this truth.

However, to fully comprehend the message Jesus was trying to convey, we must look to the original Greek language to understand exactly what the word "Comforter" means. This title is actually a translation of the Greek word *parakletos*, which is a compound of two Greek words, *para* and *kaleo*. I am going to focus on the first part of this compound word, the word *para*.

Simply put, the word *para* means *alongside*, and it carries the idea of *near proximity* or *being very close to someone or something else*. However, this term is quite versatile and can thus be seen in a variety of contexts throughout Scripture. Let's look at several New Testament examples to glean a better sense of its meaning.

The Bible says in Luke 5:1, "And it came to pass, that, as the people pressed upon him to hear the word of God, he stood *by* the lake of Gennesaret." The word "by" in this verse is a translation of the Greek word *para*. Here it conveys Jesus' close proximity to the lake of Gennesaret. He literally stood *alongside* this lake as He preached to the multitudes. In Mark 5:21, which follows the account of Jesus casting out a legion of demons from the demoniac of the Gadarenes, this term is used in a similar way. Mark records, "And when Jesus was passed over again by ship unto the other side, much people gathered unto him: and he was *nigh unto* the sea." The phrase "nigh unto" is also a translation of the word *para*, and it tells us that so many people were pressing forward to touch Jesus that He couldn't even get away from the water's edge. He was forced to walk *alongside* the sea.

In Second Timothy 2:2, we see a different usage of the word *para*. Here Paul used it to describe his close relationship with Timothy, writing, "And the things that thou hast heard *of* me among many witnesses, the same commit thou to faithful men, who shall be able to teach others also." When Paul said, "...and the things thou has learned *of* me...," the word "of " is the Greek word *para*. This conveys powerful information regarding Paul and Timothy's relationship to one another. The elderly apostle was reminding Timothy, "You learned everything *para* me. I allowed you to get alongside of me."

As a current example from my own life, I could say that my wife is *para*, or *alongside*, me. She lives with me, talks with me, shops with me, travels with me, prays with me, pastors with me, and has reared our children with me. *She is always with me.* We are side by side, close at hand, and alongside each other all the time. When two people are close in this way, they profoundly affect each other — even to the point where they begin to share the same attitudes, feelings, personality traits, habits, and gestures. In fact, they eventually know each other so well that they don't even have to ask what the other person is thinking — *they already know.*

The spiritual mentor-disciple relationship Paul and Timothy shared was probably similar in certain ways to the kind of close relationship I just described. Paul and Timothy had walked together for many years, spreading the message of the Gospel throughout the Roman world. To some degree, Timothy no doubt had picked up some of Paul's gestures, mannerisms, and thoughts, and he probably even sounded a little like Paul when he preached. The close relationship they shared allowed the truths of Paul's life to be transferred into Timothy. That is a natural consequence of this kind of intimacy.

This level of closeness is exactly what the word *para* refers to where it is used to form the compound word *parakletos*, or "Comforter," in John 14:16 and the other three references listed above. Thus, we see that the Holy Spirit is *close by* and *alongside* each of us at all times. His relationship with us is not a distant one that requires us to beg and plead for Him to draw near. *He is always with us.*

The Holy Spirit comes to reside inside us at the very moment we receive our salvation. However, this is not the full story. The use of the word *para* in John 14:16 reveals that He also comes alongside us to assist us in our daily affairs and to bring the reality of Jesus Christ into our lives. From the moment the Holy

Spirit takes up residence in our hearts, we can continuously rely on His partnership to help us overcome any obstacles we might face in life.

In other words, when you accept Jesus as your Lord and Savior, the Holy Spirit comes into your life to provide you with the assistance Jesus would offer if He was present in the flesh. Whatever Jesus would do to assist you, that is precisely what the Holy Spirit will do. He dwells in you as a permanent Resident *and* as the most reliable Partner you'll ever have in this life. That is why some newer versions of the New Testament translate the word "Comforter" as "Standby." The word "Standby" perfectly describes the Holy Spirit's close, side-by-side position in you from which He helps, empowers, leads, and guides you every step of the way.

There is no doubt that this word *para* describes *the alongside ministry* of the Holy Spirit. Perhaps you were raised in a wonderful Bible-teaching church just as I was, but you have never experienced this kind of intimate relationship with the Holy Spirit that I am describing to you. If not, today would be a great time to lift your hands and declare, "Holy Spirit, I receive You as my side-by-side Partner!" Then get ready for a divine adventure that never stops as He takes you to ever-higher levels in Him!

My Prayer for Today

Holy Spirit, I know You live inside me, but I never understood that You are also side by side with me as my Partner in life. I have treated you like an invisible Guest, when, in reality, You have been sent to me to be at my side as my Helper and Standby in times of need. Please forgive me for overlooking and ignoring You when You have been waiting so long to assist me in life. Today I throw open my arms and my heart, and I say "Welcome, Holy Spirit" — I receive You as my side-by-side Partner who has been called alongside my life! I pray this in Jesus' name!

My Confession for Today

I confess that from this moment onward, I am wide open to the ministry of the Holy Spirit. Jesus sent the Spirit to be my Helper, and I certainly need His help. I will no longer ignore Him or disregard His presence in my life. I open my heart, mind, and soul to His ministry, and I will endeavor to recognize His voice, His leading, and His guidance, and I will strive to receive His supernatural help. I declare this by faith in Jesus' name!

Questions for You to Consider

1. Of course the Holy Spirit lives inside you! But have you experienced moments when it seemed like He was right alongside you — side by side — assisting you in decisions and actions that you needed to take? In what ways do you need to cooperate with Him more?

   _____

   _____

   _____

   _____

   _____

   _____

2. What were some of the times when you really experienced the "Standby" ministry of the Holy Spirit? Have you ever recalled those moments or shared them with someone else? Take a few minutes to tell a friend how you've experienced the ministry of the Spirit in your life.

   _____

   _____

   _____

   _____

   _____

3. After reading today's *Sparkling Gem*, what are you going to do differently to embrace the "alongside ministry" of the Holy Spirit in your life? In what area of your life do you most recognize the need for His help?

_____

_____

_____

_____

_____

_____

Day 13

The Comforter, Part 2

> *And I will pray the Father, and he shall give you another Comforter....*
>
> — **John 14:16**

The word "Comforter" is used by Jesus *four* times in the space of three chapters (*see* John 14:16, John 14:26, John 15:26, and John 16:7) to describe the ministry of the Holy Spirit. We saw that the word "Comforter" is the Greek word *parakletos*, a compound of the Greek words *para* and *kaleo*, and by looking at the word *para*, we saw that the Holy Spirit is sent to come alongside us and help us navigate through our lives. Today we are going to look at the second half of *parakletos* — the Greek word *kaleo* — in order to discern how it fits with the word *para* and how we can glean an even deeper insight into the word "Comforter."

The word *kaleo* is a Greek term that means *to beckon* or *to call*. Paul used this word in Romans 1:1 when he said he was "*called to* be an apostle of Jesus Christ." This *kaleo* kind of calling carries a sense of *strategic purpose, specific intent*, and *concrete direction*. For example, God *calls* us *to* fellowship with Him, and He *calls* unbelievers *to* repentance and salvation (*see* Matthew 9:13). Likewise, both Paul and Peter used the word *kaleo* to describe God's *call to* salvation and ministry for themselves and others (*see* Romans 1:1; 8:30; 9:11,24; 1 Corinthians 1:9; 7:15; Ephesians 4:1,4; 1 Thessalonians 2:12; Hebrews 9:15; 1 Peter 1:15; 2:9).

The apostle Paul also used the word *kaleo* to describe his *call to* apostolic ministry (*see* 1 Corinthians 15:9; Galatians 1:15; 2 Timothy 1:9). When Paul heard this divine call on the road to Damascus, he was instantly imbued with a powerful sense of direction, purpose, and destiny and received a concrete direction for his life. Thus, we see that the word *kaleo* carries the idea of *summoning forth an individual to do something very specific*. We are called *to* salvation; we are called *to* the ministry; we are called *to* service in the local church, and so on. Simply put, the call is *to* something.

Returning to Jesus' message in John 14:16, we see that since *kaleo* forms the second part of the word *parakletos* ("Comforter"), God has called the Holy Spirit to do a specific work, and this calling has given the Holy Spirit purpose and direction. You might say it has given Him a job description.

What is the calling our Heavenly Father has given to the Holy Spirit? *He is called to be our Helper in this world.* This is His chief purpose and responsibility. This is His *calling*.

Now that we've seen this important aspect of the Holy Spirit's ministry, let's take a step back for a moment and review what we've learned about the Holy Spirit thus far:

1. ***The Holy Spirit is close by us.*** We have seen that the Holy Spirit indwells and seals every believer at the moment of salvation (see Ephesians 1:13). But when Jesus referred to the Holy Spirit as the "Comforter" in John 14:16, He was specifically referring to a practical relationship with the Holy Spirit that we can experience on a daily basis. We do not need to plead or beg for the Holy Spirit to come near because He is always alongside us.

2. ***The Holy Spirit has a calling.*** Just as men and women are called to the ministry, the Holy Spirit received a specific calling from God the Father to fulfill a specific assignment in this world. Just as I, for example, am specifically called to write and to teach for the Christian community, the Holy Spirit is specifically "called" (kaleo) to come "alongside" (para) each believer at all times. This means the Holy Spirit is with you when you are in the lowest pits of despair, and He is with you when things are going well. He is with you when you to go to bed at night, and He is with you when you get up in the morning. He is with you throughout your entire day. He is with you when you pray, and He is with you when you don't pray. He is with you when you behave maturely, and He is with you through your moments of immaturity. He is with you when you go to work, to the movies, or to church. Everywhere you go, the Holy Spirit goes too.

3. ***The Holy Spirit has a job assignment.*** The Holy Spirit's job is to help us! That may include convicting us of sin, empowering us for works of ministry, imparting spiritual gifts, healing other people through us, and so on. The Holy Spirit is responsible for carrying out this heavenly mission — not according to our own fleshly demands and desires, but according to the will of God,

the One who called and sent Him to us. This means you and I can be assured that the Holy Spirit will never fail at His job of helping us because He knows that He will answer to the Father for the way He performs in His role of staying alongside to help us. We may fail to recognize Him, but He will not fail at the task the Father has given to Him.

You are probably very aware of your defects and all the areas where you need to grow. Can you imagine someone who is called specifically to be with you? That is the ministry of the Holy Spirit! His primary task is to be the *Parakletos* — *called* to be *alongside* you.

So today I ask you to receive the Holy Spirit as your Partner. Simply tell Him, "I am receiving you as my Partner. You were sent to be alongside me. You've been here all along, and I have not fully received You as I should. So today I open myself to You and embrace You, Holy Spirit. I thank You for coming alongside me and for accepting such an amazing call to be my Helper!"

My Prayer for Today

Father, my eyes are being opened to the wonderful ministry of the Holy Spirit. I am shocked that I never really understood what profound help You sent to me in the Person of the Holy Spirit as my divine Partner. My heart is simply overflowing with thankfulness that You have sent the Holy Spirit into my life to assist me wherever I am and in whatever I am doing. Now I understand that He is called by YOU to be with me all the time. Please help me to be more cognizant of His presence and to honor His holiness as He comes to assist me in life! I pray this in Jesus' name!

My Confession for Today

I declare that I receive the Holy Spirit as my Partner. I choose to acknowledge Him and to cooperate with His counsel and direction. I listen to Him; I pay attention to Him; and I obediently follow when He leads or prompts me to take action. For a long time, I didn't understand the power of this gift God gave me. But now I understand, and I will honor the Holy Spirit and His role as senior Partner in my life. I declare this by faith in Jesus' name!

Questions for You to Consider

1. Of all that you read in today's *Sparkling Gem*, what truth stood out and meant the most to you? Why did it impact you more than anything else?

_____

_____

_____

_____

_____

_____

2. From what you read today, can you verbalize what is the primary "calling" of the Holy Spirit in this world? Try to put it into your own words to see if you really understood the teaching today — and if it blessed you, why not share it with someone else?

_____

_____

_____

_____

_____

_____

3. Can you think of moments when you were made especially aware of the Holy Spirit's presence at your side to help you? What was one of the most memorable of those experiences, and what was the outcome?

_____

_____

_____

_____

_____

_____

Day 14

The Heavenly Coach

> *And I will pray the Father, and he shall give you another Comforter....*
>
> — John 14:16

Today as we discuss the ministry of the Holy Spirit, I'd like to give you my favorite translation of the word "Comforter" that encapsulates all the meaning we've learned thus far. There are many possible translations for the word "Comforter," but the one that seems to satisfy me the most is the word "coach," because it conveys the meaning of the Greek word *parakletos* so well. Jesus' words in John 14:16 could read: *"I will pray the Father, and He will give you another Coach...."*

The word "Coach" perfectly describes Jesus' role toward His disciples during the three years they had walked with Him. He had been their Leader, Teacher, Mentor, Revelator, Prophet, Miracle-Worker, Healer, Pastor, and Lord. They did nothing without Him, and *everything* they did, He had shown them how to do. He was the *center* of their lives, the *focal point* of their attention, and their Mentor in everything.

Jesus was the One who sent the disciples out to spread the message of the Gospel, and He imparted the message they preached. He gave them authority to cast out demons, and He taught them how and when to address demon spirits and lay hands on the sick. Jesus showed His disciples how to deal with religious leaders and how to conduct themselves as ministers of the Gospel. He taught them how to build a ministry and even how to handle money in the ministry (*see* Matthew 10:5-14). For three years, the disciples carefully followed the Master's orders and dared not take a step without consulting Him first. In the truest meaning of the word, Jesus had been their *Coach*.

But at that Passover Supper, Jesus was letting the disciples know it was time to leave them and fulfill His divine destiny on the Cross. So He told them, "I will pray the Father, and he will give you another Comforter...." Or as we've seen today, we can paraphrase it to say, *"I will pray the Father, and he will give you another Coach...."*

The good news is that the Holy Spirit has come to teach us everything we need to know — *if* we'll listen to Him as the disciples listened to Jesus. As we cooperate with the Holy Spirit and allow Him to do what He was sent to do in our lives, He will *coach* us as Jesus coached the disciples.

Just think! You have a Partner residing inside your heart who knows all the answers you need. He is ready to give you not only the winning game plan, but also the strength and courage you need to achieve victory!

So many people have known the Lord for years — which means the Holy Spirit has been living in their hearts all that time — yet they didn't know they were supposed to have this kind of dynamic partnership with the Holy Spirit

I'm describing. But God *wants* us to know the Holy Spirit in a personal way. He wants us to begin relying on the Holy Spirit in the same way the disciples relied on Jesus. Just as Jesus was a Coach to His disciples during His time on this earth, we must think of the Holy Spirit as *our* Coach.

So what exactly does a coach do? Let's look at a few common examples:

🌿 A baseball coach teaches you how to swing that bat and hit the ball. He shows you how to run from base to base and how to use your glove to catch the ball. He says, "Hold the bat at the base with your hands wrapped around it like this. Then when you see that ball coming, swing as hard as you can and hit that ball as far as you can!"

🌿 An acting coach teaches you how to become an actor. He will coach you on how to become more convincing, more dramatic, or more comical, and he will even teach you how to cry when tears are necessary for a certain scene.

🌿 A vocal coach will teach you how to sing, how to make your breath last longer, how to push air from your diaphragm, how to make a sound stronger, how to sing on key, and how to sing in a way that truly represents the emotional content of the music. If you make a mistake while you are practicing, a vocal coach will stop you right in the middle of a song to correct you, instruct you, and then tell you to go for it again.

Fundamentally, a coach teaches, advises, corrects, instructs, trains, tutors, guides, directs, and prepares you for your upcoming assignment. If you are new at what you are doing, his *coaching* may include a little *coaxing* as you develop your confidence. A coach will encourage you as he shows you what you did wrong so you can do it right the next time.

Furthermore, a coach isn't there to hit the ball for you, sing the note for you, or play the scene for you. He's there to coach you so *you* can hit the ball, sing the note, and perform as you should. Like an apprentice learning a new job, if you will listen carefully, the Holy Spirit will direct and guide you. He'll show you what's needed. He'll open your eyes; impress your mind with supernatural direction; bring you up by the hand; and develop, foster, improve, and "break you in" on the things of God and the things of life.

As believers, we must learn to take the Holy Spirit's advice and follow Him implicitly, taking each one of our cues from Him. He must become our Heavenly Coach, and we must learn to accept His leadership and be willing to yield and concede to His divine guidance with no objections. If we will open our hearts to the ministry of the Holy Spirit, He will do everything that Jesus did. He will coach; He will teach; and He will be a Helper. He will be there to teach us how to pack our bags, how to travel, what to say, and how to pray for the sick. He will do everything that Jesus would do, because He is a *Coach* to us in the same way that Jesus was a Coach to the disciples.

Today I urge you to open your heart to the coaching ministry of the Holy Spirit. Simply say, "Holy Spirit, be my Coach." The truth is, He was sent to be your Coach whether you recognize it or not. But as you open your heart to the Holy Spirit — listening to Him and diligently following every aspect of His instruction in His role as your Coach in life — this I can promise you: It won't be long until you look back on who you were before you made the decision to allow the Holy Spirit to be your Coach, and you'll know beyond a shadow of a doubt that your decision started a process that has *completely* changed your life!

My Prayer for Today

Father, I thank You for sending the Holy Spirit to mentor, teach, advise, correct, instruct, train, tutor, guide, direct, and prepare me for my upcoming assignment. From this moment forward I am going to start thinking of the Holy Spirit as my personal Coach. I will open my spiritual ears to listen to His instruction, I will obey what He tells me to do, and I will carefully implement the instructions I hear Him speak to my heart and mind. You sent the Holy Spirit as the ongoing divine Guide, so, I position myself as a pupil of the Holy Spirit, who is my divine Coach. I pray this in Jesus' name!

My Confession for Today

I declare by faith that I am a willing, obedient, and teachable apprentice of the Holy Spirit! He speaks to my heart, tells me what to do or what actions to take, and I do exactly what I am told to do. My courage to obey is getting stronger by the day. As a result of listening to the Holy Spirit and taking my cues from Him, I am growing in my walk with the Lord, developing more confidence and experiencing greater victories day by day! I declare this by faith in Jesus' name!

Questions for You to Consider

1. Have you ever experienced a moment when the Holy Spirit coached you on what to say or how to act in a certain situation?

   _____

   _____

   _____

   _____

   _____

   _____

2. Here's an example: Has the Holy Spirit ever led you in the way you witnessed to an unbeliever? You naturally didn't know how to do it, but word-by-word and moment-by-moment, you felt led in what to say as you shared Christ with that person? Have you experienced such a moment in your life?

   _____

   _____

   _____

   _____

   _____

   _____

3. Can you think of an area where you need to stop trying to figure everything out by yourself and just allow the Holy Spirit to start coaching you on what to say and what actions to take?

_____

_____

_____

_____

_____

_____

Day 15

You're Not a Spiritual Orphan!

> *I will not leave you comfortless: I will come to you.*
> — **John 14:18**

Have you ever felt isolated or alone in this world? If you have, just remember — you are *never* alone! Imagine how alone the disciples felt when Jesus informed them that He would soon ascend to Heaven and leave them behind on the earth!

What do you think the disciples felt when Jesus told them this? They must have wondered, *What will life be like without Jesus? How will we continue without the Master walking right alongside of us?* But it was time for Jesus to ascend to the Father and to take His place as our Great High Priest.

It was natural for the disciples to feel sorrowful. To them, it must have seemed like the end of their wonderful encounter with the Lord and with the power of God. Living and walking with Jesus was more than they had ever hoped for in this world. With Jesus at their side, their lives had been filled with adventure, excitement, joy, victory, power, healings, and miracles.

Feelings of insecurity and uncertainty would have been normal for any human beings who found themselves in the disciples' position. They had grown dependent upon the physical, visible presence of Jesus — something we've never experienced and therefore cannot fully comprehend. The thought of Jesus leaving this earth probably made the disciples feel spiritually forsaken and abandoned.

In the midst of these fears, Jesus promised His disciples, "I will not leave you comfortless..." (John 14:18). Today I want us to look at the word "comfortless" in this verse. It is taken from the Greek word *orphanos,* which is where we get the word *orphan.*

In New Testament times, the word *orphanos* described *children left without a father or mother.* In today's world, the word *orphan* has exactly the same meaning. It refers to *a child who is abandoned due to the death or desertion of a father or mother.* Once orphaned, the child is deprived of parental care, supervision, and protection — *unless* that child is placed in the custody of a blood relative or a new guardian who assumes a parental role in that child's life.

However, in New Testament times the word *orphanos* was also used in a broader sense to describe *students who had been abandoned by their teacher.* Just as children are dependent on their parents, these students were reliant on their teacher to teach them, to guide them, and to prepare them for life. But once the teacher abandoned them, they felt *deserted, forsaken, discarded, and thrown away.*

In both cases, the word *orphanos* is used to carry the same idea, whether it refers to children abandoned by their parents or students discarded by their teacher. It gives the picture of *younger, less educated, less knowledgeable people feeling deserted by those they trusted and looked to for guidance.* Jesus was a spiritual father to the disciples. He knew they were completely reliant upon Him. They couldn't make it on their own in the world without Him. This is why He promised them, *"I will not leave you like orphans."*

Jesus' words could be translated to express this idea:

> *"I will not leave you behind like orphans who have been deserted by their parents, nor will I desert you like an unfaithful teacher who walks out on his students and leaves them with no supervision or help...."*

Jesus knew the disciples couldn't make it on their own in the world. That's why He sent the Holy Spirit into the world to be their new Guardian and Teacher.

You can't make it on your own in this world either — but you don't have to, because Jesus did not abandon you! He did not desert you, walk out on you, or throw you away. When He ascended to the Father, He sent the Holy Spirit to care for you, to guide you, and to teach you. Jesus did not leave you as an orphan in this world!

So meditate on this truth today, and let it sink deep into your heart: *I'm not alone! I'm not a spiritual orphan. Jesus has given me the Holy Spirit to comfort, guide, counsel, and strengthen me in every situation of life!*

My Prayer for Today

Lord, I thank You that I am not a spiritual orphan in this world. You didn't abandon me or leave me to figure out everything on my own. You sent the Holy Spirit to be my Teacher and Guide. So right now I open my heart wide to the Holy Spirit, so He can be the Helper You sent Him to be in my life. I give You thanks for sending this divine Helper, and I ask You to teach me how to lean upon Him more and more in the course of my life. I pray this in Jesus' name!

My Confession for Today

I boldly declare that the Holy Spirit is my Helper, my Teacher, and my Guide. Everything Jesus did for the disciples, the Holy Spirit now does for me. He leads me, He teaches me, and He shows me everything the Father wants me to know. I am not a spiritual orphan! I am a child of God who is fully befriended, indwelt, empowered, and led by the Spirit of God. I declare this by faith in Jesus' name!

Questions for You to Consider

1. Can you think of a critical moment in your life when you felt abandoned and alone and turned to God for comfort and support?

   _____

   _____

   _____

   _____

   _____

   _____

2. What are some of the ways the Father has comforted you in the past?

   _____

   _____

   _____

   _____

   _____

   _____

3. Are you allowing the Holy Spirit to be your Comforter, Strengthener, and Guide?

    _____

    _____

    _____

    _____

    _____

    _____

Day 16

The Holy Spirit Wants to Place a Razor-Sharp Sword in Your Hands

> *And take the helmet of salvation, and the sword of the Spirit, which is the word of God.*
>
> — **Ephesians 6:17**

How would you like God to give you a weapon that can rip to shreds the devil's strategies against you? Well, that's exactly what He has done! Ephesians 6:17 declares that God has given you "... the sword of the Spirit, which is the word of God"!

I want you to look at the word "sword" in this verse. It is the Greek word *machaira* — a word that exacted fear in the minds of those who heard it! You see, this wasn't just a sword, but a weapon of murder that caused the victim horrid pain as he lay bleeding to death.

Just for your knowledge, there were various types of swords used by the Roman army during New Testament times. For instance, there was a huge *double-handed sword* — a sword so massive that it could only be utilized with the use of *two hands*. This sword could not be used in real combat because it was too huge. Instead, it was used during sword practice sessions because it helped develop stronger muscles as soldiers swung it against a post that represented an enemy.

There was also a long sword that was used for fighting in a battle, similar to the sword we are familiar with today. This sword was very effective in battle, but it more often wounded the enemy than it killed him. Because it was long, it was most often swung at an enemy from the side, thus scraping or cutting a gouge into the side or limbs of an adversary.

But the weapon referred to in Ephesians 6:17, coming from the Greek word *machaira*, was neither of these swords. This sword was an exceptionally brutal weapon. Although it could be up to nineteen inches in length, most often it was shorter and shaped like a dagger-type sword.

Just as a dagger is inserted into a victim at close range, this sword was used only in close combat. It was razor sharp on both sides of the blade. The tip of the sword often turned upward; sometimes it was even twisted, similar to a cork screw. Because this dagger-type sword was razor sharp, it could easily be thrust into the abdomen of an adversary. And if it had a cork-screw tip, the attacker could shred the insides of a victim by twisting the sword.

All these characteristics made the *machaira* a very deadly and frightful weapon. This two-edged, dagger-type sword inflicted a wound far worse than any other sword that was available to the Roman soldier at that time. Although the other swords were deadly, this one was a terror to the imagination!

By using the word *machaira* in Ephesians 6:17, the apostle Paul is saying that God has given the Church of Jesus Christ a weapon that is frightful to the devil and his forces. Why is this weapon so horrific to the kingdom of darkness? Because it has the razor-sharp power to slash our demonic foes to shreds!

Because the word *machaira* denoted a sword that was dagger-shaped, it tells us that the "sword of the Spirit" is a weapon that is normally employed in closer combat. Let's take this one step further, so we can understand why this is so.

Notice that this verse calls it "the sword of the Spirit, which is the word of God." The term "word" is taken from the Greek word *rhema*, which describes *something that is spoken clearly and vividly, in unmistakable terms and in undeniable language.* In the New Testament, the word *rhema* carries the idea of a *quickened word*.

Here's an example of a *rhema* or a *quickened word*: You are praying about a situation when suddenly a Bible verse rises from within your heart. In that moment, you know that God has supernaturally made you aware of a verse you can stand on and claim for your situation. When this happens, it's as if the Holy Spirit has put a sword in your hand — a spiritual dagger — that you can insert into the heart of the enemy to bring about his defeat.

There are many examples of God giving someone this kind of *quickened word* in the Bible, but the best one is found in Luke 4, where Jesus is being tempted by the devil in the wilderness. Over and over again, the devil tempted and tested Jesus. But with each temptation, a scripture was *quickened* inside Jesus, and He would speak forth that scripture to the devil, brandishing it like a sword against His enemy. Each time Jesus used a verse that the Spirit had *quickened* to Him, the sword of the Word dealt a serious blow to the enemy — causing the devil to eventually flee in defeat.

Because of the words *machaira* and *rhema*, Ephesians 6:17 conveys this impression:

> *"The Spirit will place a razor-sharp sword at your disposal anytime the enemy gets too close. This sword's power will be available the very moment the Spirit quickens a specific word for a specific situation you are facing."*

When you receive a *rhema* from the Lord, the Holy Spirit drops a word or scripture into your heart, causing it to come alive supernaturally and impart special power and authority to you. This quickened word is so powerful that it is like a sword has been placed in your hands! That's why Paul calls it "the sword of the Spirit, which is the Word of God."

The next time you find yourself in close combat with the enemy, take the time to get quiet in your heart and listen. The Holy Spirit will reach up from within your spirit and *quicken* to you a scripture that has the exact power you need for the situation you find yourself in at that moment. In other words, the Holy Spirit will give you a *rhema* — a specific word for a specific time and a specific purpose.

When that happens, you have just received real "sword power" in the realm of the Spirit. It's time for you to *insert*, *twist*, and *do damage* to the devil. Then you can watch in jubilation as he hits the road and flees!

My Prayer for Today

Lord, I know that Your Spirit has the very answer I need for any situation I may confront in life. When He speaks to my heart, it places a razor-sharp sword in my hands that I can use against my spiritual enemies. Help me keep a sensitive ear to the Holy Spirit so I can recognize those moments when He is trying to give me a "rhema" that will put the devil on the run! I pray this in Jesus' name!

My Confession for Today

I confess that I can hear the Holy Spirit's voice when He drops a word into my heart at the exact moment I need it. Those quickened words impart special power and authority to me. They are so powerful that it is as if a sword has been placed in my hands! When I receive that kind of word from the Lord, I insert it, twist it, and do as much damage as possible to the devil until he's sorry he ever messed with me! I declare this by faith in Jesus' name!

Questions for You to Consider

1. Can you think of times in your life when you needed a *rhema* for the situation you were facing?

    _____

    _____

    _____

    _____

    _____

    _____

2. Did you turn to the Holy Spirit in those situations to listen for a quickened word?

    _____

    _____

    _____

    _____

    _____

    _____

3. What steps can you take to help make the Scriptures more readily available in your life? How would that change the situation you are in now?

_____

_____

_____

_____

_____

_____

Day 17

The Spirit of Truth

> *And I will pray the Father, and he shall give you another Comforter; that he may abide with you for ever; even the Spirit of truth....*
>
> — **John 14:16,17**

As you're learning more about the ministry of the Holy Spirit in these *Sparkling Gems*, you may have thought at some point, *Following the direction of the Holy Spirit at this deeper level is a little unsettling for me. Honestly, it sounds a little scary to stop trying to manage the situations of life and entrust myself completely to His leadership. I can't even see Him! What is my guarantee that I can understand how to hear or to follow Him when the Holy Spirit attempts to lead me?*

These are reasonable questions to ask if you're not used to the idea of partnering with the Holy Spirit. In fact, when Jesus first told His disciples about the ministry of the Holy Spirit, similar doubts were probably swirling around in their minds. That's why Jesus made sure to take the time during His last night on earth to assuage their fears and give them a divine guarantee regarding the ministry of the Holy Spirit. In John 14:16 and 17, He said, "And I will pray the Father, and he shall give you another Comforter; that he may abide with you for ever; even the Spirit of Truth...."

Notice that Jesus called the Holy Spirit "the Spirit of Truth" in this verse. This is the first of *three instances* where Jesus refers to the Holy Spirit as "the Spirit of Truth" over the course of His teaching in John chapters 14-16 (*see* John 15:26 and John 16:13). *Three different times in three chapters!* By repeating this phrase over and over again, Jesus was driving a truth into His disciples' hearts — that the Holy Spirit is utterly trustworthy and would never mislead them or misguide them.

In each instance where Jesus referred to the Holy Spirit as "the Spirit of Truth," the word "truth" is a translation of the Greek word *alethes*, which describes *something that can be depended upon* or *something that is trustworthy, reliable, and true*. In the Old Testament Septuagint, this term often denotes something that is *faithful, sure, stable, and firm*, as opposed to something that is unreliable and uncertain. In addition, the word *alethes* is used in the gospels to depict *the uncovering of truth* as opposed to the deliberate hiding of truth. Taken together, these meanings emphatically show that Jesus promised the Holy Spirit would *always* be trustworthy, reliable, and true. The disciples could rest assured that the Holy Spirit would never deliberately conceal information from them that was vital for them to know.

When Jesus used the word *truth* to describe the Holy Spirit, it was the equivalent of saying, "You don't need to worry that He will lead you astray or that He will lead you wrongly. You can depend upon Him and you can trust Him."

Jesus wanted the disciples to relax and understand that they could depend on the Holy Spirit to lead them correctly.

Many believers have a hard time following the leading of the Holy Spirit because they can't see Him or physically hear His voice. They say, "Oh, how I wish Jesus was here" or, "I wish Jesus would step through the door and tell me what to do in this situation."

But this way of thinking isn't in line with the Bible. It is time for you to rejoice that you have the Holy Spirit in your life because He will never mislead you! You may need to develop your ability to listen, but the Holy Spirit will always guide you to where you need to be. *He is the Spirit of Truth!* This means you can be sure that when the Holy Spirit nudges your heart to do something, it is the right thing to do. When He puts a thought into your mind, it is a right idea. When He guides your spirit, He knows something you don't and is trying to lead you on the best possible path through the obstacles in your life. He is always the Spirit of Truth, and as the Spirit of Truth, you can rely on the fact He will never mislead you.

The bottom line is this: If we're going to experience real, supernatural Christian living, we must come to a place of surrender to the Holy Spirit. He is always trying to coach and direct us, even when we're not listening. He is always as close as our next breath, dwelling in our spirits — speaking, directing, encouraging, and trying to help us make the correct decisions in life. Whether or not we listen to Him, He is still there on the inside of us because that's the job assignment He received from the Father. So to the extent we decide to listen to our Heavenly Coach and follow His advice, that is the extent we benefit from the Holy Spirit's role in our lives.

We must learn to trust the Holy Spirit's leadership and do what He instructs us to do. He is a divine Coach sent by God to help us. For Him to help us, it requires our ears, our hearts, our trust, and our obedience. Anything short of this will produce inferior results, results far short of the supernatural life you really desire. Since He is the Spirit of truth, it means He is completely trustworthy— so put aside your fears and objections and begin to let Him do His job of coaching you. This is Jesus' guarantee!

My Prayer for Today

Father, I confess that I have been fearful about following the leadership of the Holy Spirit. Today I admit it; I confess it; and I turn from it. I want to experience the coaching ministry of the Holy Spirit in my life. The Holy Spirit is the Spirit of Truth. Therefore, I know He will never mislead me. Starting today, I choose to put aside my apprehensions and surrender to the leadership of the Holy Spirit. With Him helping me, I will begin to follow His leading and let Him guide me through life. I pray this in Jesus' name!

My Confession for Today

I confess that when the Holy Spirit inspires a thought in my mind to do something, it is right. When He nudges my spirit to do something, I can rest assured that He sees and knows something I don't know and is trying to guide and direct me according to truth. He is always the Spirit of Truth and will never mislead me. I long for real, supernatural Christian living, so I confess by faith that I will surrender to the Holy Spirit. In this act of surrender, I give Him permission to be my Heavenly Coach and Counselor. I declare this by faith in Jesus' name!

Questions for You to Consider

1. Have you ever really trusted the Holy Spirit's leadership in your life, or do you typically question whether or not you should do the things He has nudged you to do?

_____

_____

_____

_____

_____

2. If you have been afraid to follow His leadership in the past, what belief about the Person of the Holy Spirit caused you to be fearful?

_____

_____

_____

_____

_____

3. Can you think of a time when you ignored the Holy Spirit's nudge in your heart, only to discover later that it really was the leading of the Holy Spirit?

_____

_____

_____

_____

_____

4. What was that experience, and what was the result of your not doing what He was prompting you to do?

_____

_____

_____

_____

_____

Day 18

The Glorifying Ministry of the Holy Spirit

> *He shall glorify me: for he shall receive of mine, and shall shew it unto you.*
>
> — **John 16:14**

Do you find the ability to express yourself in worship to God *easy* or *difficult*? Is it easy for you to lift your arms and audibly worship the Lord, or do you feel self-conscious and think about the possibility that people might be watching you? Do you hesitate to worship in the presence of others but find it easy to worship at home when no one is watching?

As Jesus prepared to depart from this world and sat in that upper room teaching His disciples about the Holy Spirit and His various roles, one of these roles He stressed that the Holy Spirit would carry out is *the ministry of glorifying Jesus*.

Jesus said in John 16:14: "He shall glorify me: for He shall receive of mine, and shall shew it unto you."

The word "glorify" is the Greek word *doxadzo,* which can be translated in a variety of ways depending on its context. It can be rendered *to extol, to praise, to magnify, to worship, to give honor, to give adulation,* or *to express one's fame or repute,* and in John 16:14, it actually encompasses the full range of these meanings.

Thus, when Jesus said, "He [the Holy Spirit] shall glorify me...," He expressly meant that the Holy Spirit's role is to *extol, magnify, glorify,* and *worship* Him. In fact, one of the Holy Spirit's chief roles is to give *adulation* and *fame* to Jesus — to *glorify* that name that is exalted above every other name (*see* Philippians 2:9). The Spirit of God doesn't seek to draw attention to Himself in any way. Rather, He points everyone toward Jesus and leads us in rapturous worship of our exalted Savior. Because the Holy Spirit is an invisible, non-material Spirit Being, He cannot glorify Jesus in the way the Lord desires without using someone as a vessel through which to work. By now, I'm sure you can guess that the vessel He chooses is the one in which He lives — *you*! How does the Holy Spirit fulfill His responsibility to glorify Jesus through you? He heals the sick, casts out demons, leads lost people to a saving knowledge of Jesus, and so on. However, one of the most effective, magnificent avenues through which He glorifies Jesus is in those moments when your heart is full, your hands are raised, and your whole being is caught up in worshiping Jesus the Lord.

By His very nature, the Holy Spirit is a *Glorifier* and a *Worshiper,* and when He is free to work in your life as a believer, it's very obvious because you *will* glorify Jesus. If you will allow the Holy Spirit to be loosed inside your life, you will find yourself wanting to throw your hands in the air, move your feet, and lift your voice to Heaven with praise and worship — completely oblivious to who might be watching or judging you. The Holy Spirit seeks to glorify Jesus in every aspect of your life, including your conversations, your behavior, and your relationships. He wants your lips to be filled with *Jesus, Jesus, Jesus.*

The Holy Spirit's primary task is to reveal Jesus to you — and He'll take you to Jesus on a level that you've never known before. He's just waiting for you to surrender and to take the plunge into this spiritual experience. Believe me when I tell you that you'll never be the same. If you've had a hard time abandoning yourself in worship in the past, today is the day for you to begin. I urge you to take a moment right now and pray, "Holy Spirit, You are a Worshiper, so I yield to You. I ask You to help me remove all my inhibition as I do. I ask You not only to glorify Jesus in my behavior, my conversations, and my life, but right now in a time of worship, I ask You to glorify Jesus through me."

If you prayed this prayer, just yield to the Holy Spirit and watch what He will do in you. Right now while no one is watching, lift your arms to Heaven and begin to express your thanksgiving to Jesus. Allow the Holy Spirit to fill you and take you into a realm of worship that you've never known before.

The Holy Spirit's primary task is to reveal Jesus to you — and if you let Him, He'll take you to Jesus on a level that you've never known before. He is there with you in this moment, and He's just waiting for you to surrender and to take the plunge into this spiritual experience. *The time and place for you to start is right now in the privacy of your own home.* He's waiting for you — *so why not start today*?

My Prayer for Today

Father, I thank You that the Holy Spirit reveals Jesus — and I ask You to help me abandon my inhibitions and enter into the freedom of worship. I know that there are realms of worship that I have never experienced, but today I am opening myself to those realms and asking that the Holy Spirit unleash worship in me as never before. I surrender myself to be an instrument of worship and, Holy Spirit, I ask You to take me on an adventure as I learn to worship Jesus as You reveal Him to me on a level I've never experienced before. I pray this in Jesus' name!

My Confession for Today

I declare that my entire body — all that I am — is an instrument that the Holy Spirit uses to magnify and to exalt the name and Person of Jesus Christ. Inhibitions have no part in my worship. I am free to express my adoration and love for Jesus — the One who is higher than all others and whose name is more highly exalted than any other name. Inhibitions must go from me in Jesus' name, for I am liberated to worship Jesus in the power of the Holy Spirit! I declare this by faith in Jesus' name!

Questions for You to Consider

1. Has there been a moment when you threw off all restraint and worshiped Jesus in the power of the Holy Spirit? When did that experience occur, and has anything stopped you from entering into that type of worship again?

_____

_____

_____

_____

_____

_____

2. What happened inside you when you threw off those restraints and fully entered into the worship of Jesus? What did the Holy Spirit do inside you that changed you forever?

_____

_____

_____

_____

_____

_____

3. What would you say to someone who has never experienced freedom in worship? What has it done for you, and what will it do for them?

_____

_____

_____

_____

_____

_____

Day 19

A Spirit of Wisdom and Revelation for You

> *That the God of our Lord Jesus Christ, the Father of glory, may give unto you the spirit of wisdom and revelation in the knowledge of him.*
>
> — **Ephesians 1:17**

Would you like to receive guidance from the Holy Spirit to help you make some important decisions today? If so, Paul's prayer to the Ephesian church in Ephesians 1:17 is an important scripture for you to apply to your own life.

The word "wisdom" in this verse is from the Greek word *sophias*. It is an old Greek word that was used to describe *insight* or *wisdom not naturally attained*. In other words, this is not natural human wisdom — this is *special insight*.

The word "revelation" is from the word *apokalupsis*. It refers to *something that has been veiled or hidden for a long time and then suddenly, almost instantaneously, becomes clear and visible to the mind or eye.* It is like pulling the curtains out of the way so you can see what has always been just outside your window. The scene was always there for you to enjoy, but the curtains blocked your ability to see the real picture. But when the curtains are drawn apart, you can suddenly see what has been hidden from your view. The moment you see beyond the curtain for the first time and observe what has been there all along but not evident to you — *that* is what the Bible calls a "revelation."

Now apply the meaning of this word to the realm of spiritual truths. The truths we now grasp and enjoy were always there in the realm of the Spirit, but they were veiled — *hidden* to us. It wasn't the time for these truths to be revealed yet, so they remained obscured from our sight, even though they were always there. But once the right time came and the Holy Spirit removed the veil that obstructed our view, our minds instantly saw and understood. When this occurred, you and I had a *revelation*!

Can you remember times in your past when you suddenly saw something in the Bible you had never seen before? That truth had been there all along, but it had been hidden to your eyes. Then suddenly one day, it was as if someone pulled the covers off that verse, and it literally jumped off the pages in front of you. You saw it! You *understood* it! You had a *revelation*!

It is a fact that truths remain hidden until God chooses to reveal them to us. This is why Paul prayed for God "to give" the Ephesian church a spirit of wisdom and revelation. The phrase "to give" is the Greek word *didomi*, which means *to hand something over completely to someone else.* It could also be translated *to impart*.

Because the Ephesian church needed wisdom beyond their own human understanding, Paul asked God to give them what they needed: *special insight that is not naturally attained.* Then Paul clarified what he meant by adding the word "revelation." One expositor has said the verse could be better translated to "give unto you a spirit of wisdom, *even revelation*!"

Taking all this into consideration, Ephesians 1:17 could be translated:

> *"That the God of our Lord Jesus Christ, the Father of glory, may give you special insight — I'm talking about wisdom that is not naturally attained. This is the divine moment when the curtains are drawn back, and you are supernaturally enabled to see what you could never see by yourself...."*

God had all the answers the Ephesian believers needed. By themselves, they would never have been smart enough to figure it all out. So Paul besought God to impart to them the wisdom they needed. Then Paul clarified that this kind of wisdom would only come to them *by revelation* — which only God can give.

If you need direction and guidance today, stop right now and pray Paul's prayer in Ephesians 1:17 for your own life. Ask God to give you "the spirit of wisdom and revelation." God has all the answers you need, and they're not as far from you as you may think. In one moment, He can remove the veil of ignorance and help you see clearly the things you need to understand. *All you have to do is ASK!*

My Prayer for Today

Lord, I ask You to give me the insight and wisdom I need for this moment in my life. There is so much I need to know, but I am unable to figure it all out by myself. Today I ask that the Holy Spirit would take away the veil that has obscured my view. I ask that my eyes be opened to see exactly what I need to know. I ask You to give me a real revelation about my life, my situation, and the truth I need to know right now. I pray this in Jesus' name!

My Confession for Today

I boldly declare that God gives me "the spirit of wisdom and revelation" regarding the truth I need in my life right now. God has all the answers I need — answers I will not find with my own natural reasoning. At the right moment, the Holy Spirit will remove the veil of ignorance that has blinded my view and help me see clearly the things I need to understand. I declare this by faith in Jesus' name!

Questions for You to Consider

1. Can you remember a time in your life when a light bulb went off in your spirit and you saw a new revelation from God that you'd never seen before?

   _____

   _____

   _____

   _____

   _____

   _____

2. What difficult issues in your life have you been trying to work out in your own strength? Write them down.

   _____

   _____

   _____

   _____

   _____

3. Are you ready to surrender those issues to God and ask Him to reveal to you the answers you need?

_____

_____

_____

_____

_____

_____

Day 20

The Holy Spirit — a Partner Who Wants to Take Responsibility for You in This Life!

> *The grace of the Lord Jesus Christ, and the love of God, and the communion of the Holy Ghost, be with you all. Amen.*
>
> — **2 Corinthians 13:14**

Most all of us would say we want to live a victorious Christian life. But without daily communion with the Holy Spirit, it's impossible to attain that goal. Communion with the Holy Spirit is the launching pad for a life of supernatural power and consistency.

In Second Corinthians 13:14, Paul says, "The grace of the Lord Jesus Christ, and the love of God, and the communion of the Holy Ghost, be with you all. Amen." I want you to notice the word "communion" in this verse, because *communion with the Spirit* is what we are talking about today. The word "communion" is the Greek word *koinonia,* a word that has a whole flavor of meanings, but one primary meaning is that of *partnership.*

An example of *koinonia* conveying the idea of partnership can be found in Luke 5:7 after Jesus supplied a miraculous catch of fish. After the fishermen had fished all night and caught nothing, Jesus told them to cast their nets on the other side. When they obeyed, they caught such a massive amount of fish that the nets began to break!

Peter knew he couldn't handle this miraculous catch by himself, so he called to other fishermen in nearby boats to come and assist him. Luke 5:7 says, "And they beckoned unto their *partners*, which were in the other ship, that they should come and help them. And they came, and filled both the ships, so that they began to sink."

Do you see the word "partners" in this verse? It is a form of this word *koinonia*. However, in Luke 5:7 it refers to real, legitimate business partners. One scholar says that this word used in this context lets us know that Peter was no small-time fisherman. He owned an entire fishing enterprise, and those men in the other boats were his *business associates* or his *company partners*. Whether these other fishermen were co-owners or employees who worked for Peter, they were all working together on the same job and were focused on a joint venture to catch and sell fish.

Keeping this in mind, Second Corinthians 13:14 could convey the following idea: *"...and the PARTNERSHIP of the Holy Spirit be with you all."*

If you stop and think about it, this really makes a lot of sense. When Jesus' earthly ministry was in operation, He and the Holy Spirit always worked together. Jesus was *conceived* of the Holy Spirit (Luke 1:35); *empowered* by the Holy Spirit (Matthew 3:16); and *led* by the Holy Spirit (Matthew 4:1). Jesus also healed people by the power of the Holy Spirit (Acts 10:38); cast out demons by the power of the Holy Spirit (Matthew 12:28); was *resurrected* from the dead by the power of the Holy Spirit (Romans 8:11); and was seated at God's right hand in the heavenly places through the power of the Holy Spirit (Ephesians 1:19,20).

Every time we see Jesus in the Gospels, He is working hand in hand with the Holy Spirit. In fact, Jesus even said He wouldn't initiate anything by Himself, indicating His total dependence on the Spirit of God (John 5:30). Well, if Jesus needed this kind of ongoing partnership with the Holy Spirit in order to accomplish His divine role in the earth, we certainly have to have it as well!

But there is yet another idea conveyed by the word "communion" (*koinonia*) — that is, the idea of *taking responsibility for someone*. An example of this is found in Philippians 4:14, when Paul wrote to the Philippians and commended them for the generous gift they sent for his ministry. He told them, "Notwithstanding ye have well done, that ye did *communicate* with my affliction." The word "communicate" here is another use of the word *koinonia*.

At the time Paul wrote the Philippian letter, he was in prison in Rome. Over the years, he had traveled and preached, raised up churches, worked with leaders, and given his life for the Church. But of all the churches Paul had poured his life into, none of them helped him financially the way they should have.

In order to cover his expenses, Paul worked as a tentmaker during the day; then he preached and trained leaders during the evenings. This wasn't the best plan, but because no one would support him, it was what he had to do. He was pouring his heart and soul into churches that were not financially helping him bear his load.

Paul was in prison in Rome when he received a special delivery letter from the Philippians. In that package, he found a sizable offering that the Philippian church had sent to support him during his time of difficulty. In other words, the Philippian church didn't just say, "We'll pray for your situation, Brother," and then forget about Paul. Instead, they understood their responsibility to help him, so they took up an offering to support him and to communicate their love for him. In other words, they took *responsibility* for him. Paul uses the Greek word *koinonia* to convey this meaning — the same word he uses in Second Corinthians 13:14 when he writes about the "communion of the Holy Spirit."

Thus, Second Corinthians 13:14 could also be read this way: "...and the RESPONSIBILITY of the Holy Spirit be with you all."

This means that just as the Holy Spirit wants to become your Partner, He also wants to assume great responsibility for you in this world. If you wish, He'll stand by and watch you try to do it all alone. But if you'll open your heart to the Spirit of God, He will assume a more active role in your life. He wants you to know that you are not alone — and that He will take *responsibility* for you!

If the cry of your heart is to know the *partnership* and the *responsibility* of the Holy Spirit — not merely as mental doctrines, but as constant, daily realities in your life — then decide today to get to know the Holy Spirit as your intimate Friend. Make Him your Partner. Allow Him to help you fulfill the responsibilities of your calling in Christ.

Begin today to develop a walk of daily communion with the Greater One within. Let Him be all He wants to be in your life — your Source of wisdom, power, and strength to launch you forth into victory!

My Prayer for Today

Holy Spirit, I want to thank You for being my Partner in this world. I need Your partnership. I know that without You, I am so limited in what I am able to do. You see what I can't see; You know what I don't know; You have wisdom and insight that I don't have. I simply must have Your help if I am going to do what God has asked me to do. I ask You to please forgive me for all the times I have gotten in such a hurry that I didn't take time to fellowship with You. From this moment on, I promise I will do my best to consult You before I make a decision or take a single step! I pray this in Jesus' name!

My Confession for Today

I confess that I am led by the Spirit of God. I am careful not to make big decisions without consulting Him first. The Holy Spirit is my Leader, my Teacher, and my Guide; therefore, I look to Him to help me make the right decisions and take the right actions in every sphere of my life — my family, my business, and my ministry. Every day I experience more and more victory because I allow the Holy Spirit to direct all my steps. I declare this by faith in Jesus' name!

Questions for You to Consider

1. Have you asked the Spirit of God to be your Partner in life and to take responsibility for all your cares and concerns?

    _____

    _____

    _____

    _____

    _____

    _____

2. What can you do to make the Holy Spirit a closer, more active Partner in every area of life?

    _____

    _____

    _____

    _____

    _____

    _____

3. Have you spent quality time in communion with the Holy Spirit today, being still and simply knowing that He is your God?

_____

_____

_____

_____

_____

_____

Day 21

God's Spirit Dwells in You!

> *Know ye not that ye are the temple of God, and that the Spirit of God dwelleth in you?*
>
> — 1 Corinthians 3:16

When we first started our church in Moscow in the year 2000, God moved supernaturally in our church's midst, and our congregation miraculously began to grow by leaps and bounds. It wasn't long before the auditorium we had rented was filled to maximum capacity, and we still needed room for more people. So we rented a bigger auditorium — but once again, soon we were at capacity. This happened again and again over the years.

In addition, because our church membership was growing so rapidly, it soon meant we needed a larger office to accommodate the business end of things, and so the search began. After a period of looking, we finally secured an office in an ideal location. It was directly in the center of downtown Moscow — a two-minute walk from the *Bolshoi Theatre* and a short seven-minute walk from *Red Square*. You couldn't get any closer to the heart of the city than this location. It was *ideal* in every way!

Because of the building's prime location, I knew that many high-ranking visitors would come to this office to meet with our ministry. Therefore, our space needed to be decorated professionally and beautifully to make a first-class impression of the Gospel on every person who entered that office. To this end, Denise and I worked hard to choose the perfect wallpaper, carpet, and furniture to adorn our church office. Finally, the day came when the interior decorating work was to commence on the new office. The first work to be done that day was to hang the wallpaper Denise and I had so carefully chosen. We were so excited to see how it would transform the "look" of that office!

The reception area was the first room in our office to be wallpapered. This was the most important part of our office because it was where people's first impressions of our ministry would be made. Many people in this region of the world have historically ridiculed people of faith, so it was essential to us that our guests associate excellence with the name of Jesus Christ as they entered our reception area. Therefore, we chose an elegant, intricate, floral-patterned wall covering for that space, and we knew it would take a real master to hang it correctly.

The person we chose to hang the wallpaper was a woman from our congregation who maintained that she was such a master at the craft. She had even volunteered to do the job and to do it for free as a gift to the church, and we were delighted. I met her at the office and showed her the wallpaper, and she got started. I left the site because I had a meeting in another part of the city, assuming this "master" would do a beautiful job. However, when I returned to see what she had done, I was *shocked*!

She had hung a lot of paper and had done it very quickly, but none of the patterns from strip to strip matched each other. I was so stunned that for a few moments, I was literally *speechless*.

She asked me, "How do you like my job?"

I regained my composure and replied, "Do you realize none of the patterns match?"

She said, "Oh, you wanted the patterns to match? Why didn't you tell me?"

I told her, "When I heard you were a professional paper hanger, I assumed you would know to match the patterns of each strip. I'm sorry, but you'll have to take it down and start all over again."

On her second attempt, she matched the patterns, but this time the wallpaper was very visibly *crooked*. As I explained to her that this room would be a reception for very important guests and the wallpaper couldn't be crooked, she said, "But if you look at it like *this*, it doesn't look crooked." With that, she tilted her head sideways and framed the crooked wallpaper between her hands. She said, "If you tilt your head and look at it like this, it looks normal. See?"

I was astounded that she would try to tell me that it would look normal if I would just cock my head to the left. I replied, "People won't walk into this office and cock their heads sideways so the wallpaper will look normal. People will walk in here standing upright, as people do, and they will think this wallpaper looks crooked and crazy. Please tear it down, and I'll find someone else to properly hang the paper."

When I instructed this woman to rip the paper off the walls, I heard people gasping. A staff member privately suggested, "Pastor, this wallpaper is expensive. What if we just paint it and forget about it? Does it really have to be torn off the walls a second time? Do you really think anyone will notice that it's crooked? Can't we just leave it the way it is instead of losing money?"

I finally had to walk over to the wall and begin tearing the paper off myself — as everyone around me gazed in shock. The sound of expensive paper being ripped from the walls filled the ears of all who stood by. Piece by piece, the wallpaper fell to the ground. When I saw people staring in disbelief at what I was doing, I turned and explained to them, "This room is designed for guests. Nothing less than our best is acceptable. I want every person who enters this room to sense that we care about them and have prepared a place for them that is special and shows them respect."

That day my staff finally realized how important it was to me that we do our best to make guests feels honored and welcomed. But as important as it was for me to treat the guests of our ministry with respect, it is far more important that we do our very best to make *God* welcome in our lives.

In First Corinthians 3:16, the apostle Paul wrote, "Know ye not that ye are the temple of God, and that the Spirit of God dwelleth in you?" This word "dwelleth" is the Greek word *oikeo*, which denotes a *house.* However, the word *oikeo* as used by Paul in this verse means *to dwell in* or *to take up residency in a house.* This means God is not like a guest who comes and goes. Rather, when a person repents and comes to Christ, God's Spirit moves in and takes up residence. In other words, that newly saved believer's heart becomes the Holy Spirit's *permanent home.*

When a believer first accepts Christ as his Lord and Savior, there are areas in his life that need to be healed, restored, and changed. By walking in obedience to the Word of God and learning to serve in the local church, a person's mind can become conformed to the mind of Christ, and his life can gradually become transformed to reflect the excellence of Jesus Christ. However, for these changes to occur in a person's life, it requires his complete participation. These kinds of changes don't occur without hard work, commitment, and determination to make one's heart a place where God feels honored.

Never forget that God's Spirit — *the Spirit of holiness* — now lives inside you. What are you doing to make Him feel welcome? Are you allowing the crooked and mismatched places of your life to remain unchecked, or are you doing your best to rip them away, one piece at a time, so you can make your heart a place that shows God honor and respect?

It's great that we do so much to make guests feel welcomed in our homes, churches, or offices. But think about how much more important it is that we build our lives in such a way that conveys to God just how thankful we are that He dwells in our hearts!

God has moved into your heart and made it His permanent home. Don't you think you should "hang the wallpaper" in your heart in such a way that it shows Him how happy and honored you are that He is there?

My Prayer for Today

Lord, I thank You for coming to live permanently in my heart. What a miracle it is that You would want to live in someone like me. I am amazed and dumbfounded by this great act of grace — and my heart is overwhelmed with thankfulness that You have chosen to make my heart Your home. I know that I have a lot of areas in my life that need attention, and I'm asking You to give me the grace and power to deal with each of these areas one step at a time. Without Your help, I can't change myself. But with Your grace working inside me, I can be conformed to think with the mind of Christ, and my behavior can be transformed to reflect the character of Christ. I thank You in advance for helping me get rid of all the crooked and mismatched places in my soul so I can become a dwelling place where You are comfortable to abide. I pray this in Jesus' name!

My Confession for Today

I confess that I obey the instructions of the Holy Spirit as He guides me to correct all the crooked and mismatched places in my mind, my soul, and my character. God's Spirit lives in me, and He is giving me the insight, wisdom, and strength to peel flawed areas away from my life so I can become a shining example of what Jesus desires His people to be. By myself I cannot change. But thank God, the Holy Spirit who lives within gives me the power to confront every area of my life that needs to be brought into alignment with His perfect will. His strength is MY strength to make wrong things right. I can do all things through Christ who strengthens me, as He continually helps me become all that He wants me to be! I declare this by faith in Jesus' name!

Questions for You to Consider

1. Can you think of specific parts of your life that are intolerable and hurtful to God's Spirit, but that you have allowed to continue in your life? What are the areas in your life that you know are wrong and God is asking you to change? Why don't you make a list of these areas and keep it nearby so you can be reminded of the changes you need to implement as you pray each day?

   _____

   _____

   _____

   _____

   _____

2. What do you do in your life that especially makes God feel welcomed, honored, and respected?

   _____

   _____

   _____

   _____

   _____

3. If you were God and were looking for a heart that made you feel welcomed, honored, and respected, what qualities would you be looking for that let you know you were truly wanted?

_____

_____

_____

_____

_____

_____

Day 22

The Permanent Indweller of Your Heart

> *Do ye think that the scripture saith in vain, The spirit that dwelleth in us lusteth to envy?*
>
> — James 4:5

According to James 4:5, the Holy Spirit came into our hearts as a Permanent Indweller. It says, "Do ye think that the scripture saith in vain, The spirit that *dwelleth* in us lusteth to envy?"

The Greek word for "dwelleth" is *katoikidzo*, a compound of the words *kata* and *oikos*. The word *kata* carries the idea of *settling down*, and the word *oikos* is the word for a *house*. Taken together, the new word means *to take up residency* or *to dwell in a house*. This word carries the idea of *residing permanently*. In other words, this word would never describe a transient or one who came to live in a place only temporarily. This is the picture of a person who has settled into a home with no intention of *ever* leaving.

In other words, when the Holy Spirit came to live in you, it wasn't for a short period of time. When He came, He came to *stay*. From the moment you made Jesus your Savior and Lord, the Holy Spirit made your heart His permanent home. He has, so to speak, hung His own pictures on the walls, moved His furniture in, and settled down into a nice, big comfortable chair. He has no intention of ever moving out to leave your heart vacant while He finds somewhere else to live.

Think of that! The Holy Spirit doesn't come only to visit occasionally. Your heart is His *home*. Meditate on this truth, and determine to live each moment of the day with a deep sense of awareness of the Holy Spirit's indwelling presence. Welcome His fellowship; talk to Him; and yield to Him as He prays through you and gives you guidance and direction. A deeper realization of the Permanent Indweller who lives on the inside of you will help you stay on track and continually move forward in your walk in Christ!

My Prayer for Today

Holy Spirit, I am so thankful that my heart is Your home! I worship You for taking up residency inside of me! The thought is almost too glorious for my mind to comprehend! I welcome Your fellowship. Teach me how to talk with You, yield to You, and cooperate with You as You pray through me, giving me guidance and direction every day. I ask You to please open my understanding to a deeper realization of Your permanent indwelling so I stay on track spiritually and continually move forward in my walk in Christ! I pray this in Jesus' name!

My Confession for Today

I am thankful to declare that the Holy Spirit is not a guest who occasionally comes to visit me. He moved into my recreated spirit to permanently abide with me. He regenerated and renovated me, and He brought His power and glory along with Him when He moved inside me. I am the permanent home for the Spirit of God. I declare this by faith in Jesus' name!

Questions for You to Consider

1. Since your heart is the home of the Holy Spirit, what do you need to do to make Him feel more comfortable there? What changes do you need to make to accommodate His holy presence?

   _____

   _____

   _____

   _____

   _____

2. So many times I've heard songs that invite the Holy Spirit to come and visit us, but that isn't even scriptural! He lives *inside* us. We are not a temporary place He comes to visit. Can you think of songs that might be unscriptural along these lines that we sang with all of our hearts in the past, not realizing we were singing unscriptural songs?

   _____

   _____

   _____

   _____

   _____

3. A guest in a hotel doesn't have many rights, but when you *live* in a house permanently, it becomes *your home* and you have rights there. What kind of rights does the Holy Spirit have as a Permanent Indweller in your heart?

_____

_____

_____

_____

_____

Day 23

The Holy Spirit Is Like Wind

> *And suddenly there came a sound from heaven as of **a rushing mighty wind**, and it filled all the house where they were sitting.*
>
> — **Acts 2:2**

Having grown up in Oklahoma, my family members were all well aware of the power of the wind. If atmospheric conditions were right, we'd hear the city sirens begin to blare — warning everyone to run for cover because severe winds or a tornado was imminent. At the sound of those sirens, I remember my mother commanding me to get off the porch and into the house to seek shelter. Running for cover was the last thing I wanted to do, because I loved watching how the low-level clouds would suddenly turn eerily dark. The latent power of wind simply mesmerized me. The fact that the wind could not be seen but could be felt — and the added fact that it was so unpredictable — made me want to stay on the porch so I could feel the wind in action.

But at my mother's urging, I would eventually head for cover with the rest of the family, usually in a small, enclosed area of the house that could potentially withstand a hit, like a bathroom or closet. We'd shut the door and wait. When the sirens stopped blaring, that's when we knew the storm had passed. Many times we emerged from our hiding place to find large tree limbs strewn across our yard that had been carried there from blocks away. Sometimes we would see huge trees that the wind had ripped up from their roots. Very often after these storms, we'd venture out to discover that roads were impassable because of debris — trees, limbs, and power lines that had been knocked down by the wind and scattered across the roads. Electrical sparks would spit fiercely into the air from where electrical lines had been severed, so we would drive around them or look for alternative routes until electric crews arrived to repair the fallen lines.

We're all aware of the potentially destructive power of wind. But if properly harnessed, wind can also bring tremendous benefits. Think how much it would impact the world if there were no wind. The earth would be stagnant, stinking from pollution and from the normal decaying process that is occurring on the planet.

Just think how essential wind has been to the very development of civilization. For example, if there were no winds, exploration never would have occurred. Consider the great ships of the past that had no mechanical or nuclear energy to drive them, yet they glided across oceans with ease as their great sails caught the winds. The world was explored and conquered by men who "set sail" and traveled the globe, fueled by the force of the wind.

In fact, if no wind were blowing, there would be no movement. Windmill blades would never turn — and the production of materials would be slowed and diminished. Wind is essential for progress to be made. Without wind, we would be hundreds of years behind where we presently are in history. Wind cannot be seen, but its effects can be felt and heard — *just like the Holy Spirit*. We cannot see Him, but we can feel the effects of His presence and His power. On the Day of Pentecost, Acts 2:2 says, "And suddenly there came a sound from heaven as of a rushing mighty wind, and it filled all the house where they were sitting." Today I want us to look at the comparison of wind to the Holy Spirit in this verse to see what we can learn about why the Spirit came in this manner on the Day of Pentecost and what this means to you and me.

In Acts 2:2, 120 disciples were gathered in the Upper Room, waiting for the promise of the Father as Jesus had commanded them (*see* Acts 1:4). The Bible says that as they were waiting, "suddenly" there came from Heaven a certain sound. The word "suddenly" was translated from the Greek word *aphno*, which carries with it the idea that something took them *off guard* and *by surprise*.

Acts 2:2 goes on to say, "...Suddenly *there came* a *sound*...." This phrase "there came" is a translation of the word *ginomai*, which in this case describes something very similar to the Greek word *aphno* — *something that happens unexpectedly or that catches one off guard*. The word "sound" in this verse is the Greek word *echos*. This is the very word that is used in Luke 21:5 to describe *the deafening roar* of the sea.

Verse 2 continues, "...A sound *from heaven*...." The phrase "from heaven" is from the Greek words *ek tou ourano*. The word *ek* means *out*, and *tou ourano* means *of Heaven*. This leaves no doubt that this sound had originated and emanated from Heaven itself.

Then Luke compared this sound from Heaven to a "rushing, mighty wind." The word "rushing" was translated from the Greek word *pheromones*, the present-passive participle of *phero*, which means to be *carried, borne*, or *driven* and agrees with the idea of *something borne or driven downward very loudly*. When this sound from Heaven came, it was *loud* — so loud that the writer used the word "rushing" to describe what Jesus' disciples heard that day in the room where they gathered.

Furthermore, the Greek text also uses the word *biaias* for "mighty," a word that could be better translated as *violent*. Hence, this "sound" thundered like the roaring of a sea or a mighty wind that swept downward very loudly and violently.

The word "wind" itself comes from *pnoe*, which describes wind so loud that one may be tempted to cover his ears from the overpowering noise of it. This means when the Spirit was poured out, it was no quiet affair. It was loud, noisy, and violent — not violent in terms of *destructive*, but rather it was *strongly felt*.

Just as wind moves ships, empowers engines, drives windmills, and disperses pollution from the earth — when the Holy Spirit moved on the Day of Pentecost, He released *power* strong enough to transform 120 disciples into a mighty force for God!

When the wind of the Spirit blows upon a near-dead church, it can blow life back into that congregation again. When all of our organizing is done and is nearly perfect, yet we still lack power, it is the wind of the Holy Spirit that can blow strongly upon us and cause a vision or organization to come alive with the life of God.

If you are someone who desires a "quiet" relationship with God, I must warn you that when the Holy Spirit's wind blows, it is rarely a quiet affair. It is usually noisy and attention-attracting — or as we've seen, it's a powerful force that sweeps downward from Heaven like the roaring of the sea.

When God formed man, He formed him perfectly. But man had no breath in his lungs until God breathed the breath of life into him (*see* Genesis 2:7). Likewise, when the Church was assembled on the Day of Pentecost, it had no power until the Holy Spirit breathed into that assembly. When that loud *"boom"* exploded overhead in the room where they were gathered, the power of God came upon 120 disciples, and they became an *empowered, mighty force* in the earth as a result.

Wind is a good word to describe the power of the Holy Spirit. Change happens when winds blow — and when the Holy Spirit moves, He brings change like wind. Energy is produced by wind — and when the Holy Spirit moves in this manner, He supplies supernatural energy. He empowers us to do what we could not naturally do on our own. *Oh, how we need the supernatural wind of the Holy Spirit!*

My Prayer for Today

Father, I thank You for the movement of the Holy Spirit that comes to empower me and to make me alive to minister and represent You on the earth! So many times I do everything that needs to be done organizationally, but life and power remain missing. Today I personally ask You to blow Your wind upon me, upon my church, and upon the mission organizations I support so they will all be "moved" by the Spirit and supernaturally empowered to do the work of the ministry! I pray this in Jesus' name!

My Confession for Today

I boldly declare that I will not be satisfied until a fresh wind of the Holy Spirit has blown upon me to give me divine life and divine energy. Without this life, I can only do what human power can do, but when the Spirit blows His divine wind upon me, suddenly I am empowered to do what I could have never done before. Today — right now — I am opening myself to the rushing mighty wind of the Holy Spirit. I confess that I am a ready recipient, and I am receiving a fresh infilling of this divine wind to empower me for God's service. I declare this by faith in Jesus' name!

Questions for You to Consider

1. Can you think of a time when you did everything naturally that could be done, but you still lacked the power to do the work of the ministry? Do you feel that way right now? If yes, what are you going to do about it after reading today's *Sparkling Gem*?

_____

_____

_____

_____

_____

2. Have you ever had a moment when the Spirit's wind moved upon you — and suddenly you were supernaturally empowered like never before in your life?

_____

_____

_____

_____

_____

3. If you know someone who feels spiritually stagnant, how would you encourage him or her after what you have read in today's *Sparkling Gem?*

_____

_____

_____

_____

_____

_____

Day 24

"Welcome to Your New Home!"

> *As they ministered to the Lord, and fasted, the Holy Ghost said, Separate me Barnabas and Saul for the work whereunto I have called them.*
>
> — **Acts 13:2**

When I made my first missions trip to the USSR, it was in the spring of 1991, just months before the Soviet Union finally dissolved. I was shocked by how dilapidated everything seemed to be. From what I observed, the mighty USSR was worn out and falling apart. The streets, sidewalks, cars, shops, people's clothing — everything I saw — simply looked either broken, exhausted, or worn out.

I checked into my hotel, and when I pulled the curtains back to give me a view of the street below, they were so rotten that they ripped right off the curtain rod into my hands. For the rest of my stay there, I had no curtains. There was a dead mouse in one corner of the room, and the shower looked like it hadn't been cleaned in decades. I was simply stunned that a global superpower that had kept the rest of the world in fear for so many years was so utterly dilapidated.

The next morning after our arrival, my teammates and I walked to the building where the first aboveground Bible school was being conducted — the first in more than 70 years. Two hundred and twenty students had gathered from every republic of the USSR to attend the school, and I wept when I realized this was a dream come true for them. They lifted their hands to worship, and the Spirit of God moved across the large classroom in a powerful manner. His presence was so strong.

When I stood in front of that room full of young people from all over the Soviet Union to teach them for the first time, I approached the lectern to begin my first teaching session, opened my Bible, took a step back, and looked up at the room full of students eagerly looking back at me. And at that moment, I vividly heard the Holy Spirit speak loudly to my heart and say, *"WELCOME TO YOUR NEW HOME!"*

I know the voice of the Holy Spirit, and there was no doubt in my heart or mind that it was the Spirit who had spoken these words to me. Feeling shocked by what I'd just heard, I choked up and stumbled with my words a bit. Then the Holy Spirit spoke it a second time: *"WELCOME TO YOUR NEW HOME!"*

With that, I *knew* God was calling me to relocate my family to the Soviet Union. As I looked at those 220 students and the dilapidated surroundings all around me, I kept thinking, *God is calling me to make THIS my home and to embrace these students and the USSR for me and my family's future.*

Later that day in prayer, the Lord continued speaking to my spirit. He explained, *"There are many good Bible teachers in the United States, but I need skilled Bible teachers HERE to undergird the massive move of My Spirit that is happening. That is why I am calling you to move here and to do it as quickly as possible.*"

This was completely contrary to the plans I had made for my life and ministry. Back in those days, we were receiving 900 invitations a year to come and hold seminars in churches and speak in conferences. The growth of our ministry was literally exploding in the United States — and my books were becoming bestsellers. I had never dreamed of moving away from America and leaving that life behind. But that was exactly what God was calling us to do. That week as I ministered every day to the students, the love of God in me connected me to them, and I could begin to visually see our family living in the USSR.

When I came back to Tulsa after that missions trip, I knew I needed to break the news to Denise. I didn't know how she would respond, but the Lord had prepared her heart before I ever said a word, and the same grace that was upon me was upon Denise. She said, "I'm not excited yet, but when we step onto that plane to move, I'll be filled with faith and anticipation." Our sons were too young to understand what the Soviet Union was, so they just exploded with glee that we were going to be doing something adventurous as we followed the will of God.

Finally, the morning came when Denise and I and our three small sons gathered at the airport with family and friends. We hugged and kissed everyone and told them all farewell; then we stepped onto the plane that would carry us to our new home in the former Soviet Union. As we sat down in those seats on the plane, Denise and I looked at each other with jubilation, because we knew we had passed a major test. We had said *yes* to the Lord, surrendering to His revealed will for us, and we were on our way to the greatest adventure of our lives.

Saying *yes* to the Lord requires surrender. I'm talking about that moment when you are willing to lay down all your own plans and yield to what the Holy Spirit has revealed to you about God's will for your life. Some people pass this test, whereas others do not. However, those who surrender, yield, and obey experience the joy, power, and victory of the Spirit. They live an enriched life filled both with opportunities to be seized and obstacles to be overcome in order to attain victory and to complete the assignment.

I want to tell you how I felt that day when the Holy Spirit said, *"WELCOME TO YOUR NEW HOME!"* It immediately reminded me of Acts 13:2, which says, "As they [the elders in Antioch] ministered to the Lord, and fasted, the Holy Ghost said, Separate me Barnabas and Saul for the work whereunto I have called them."

Barnabas and Saul had been serving in the church of Antioch for several years when suddenly during a time of prayer and fasting, the Holy Spirit said, *"Separate me Barnabas and Saul for the work whereunto I have called them."* The word "separate" is the Greek word *asphortidzo*, and it means *to mark off, to set boundaries around*, or *to set apart for a special purpose*. The verse continues to say that they were to be set apart "...for the work whereunto I have called them." Apparently, God had a "work" for these two men that exceeded what they had done in Antioch.

Serving in Antioch was an honor, but it was not the ultimate goal of God's call on their lives. Way beyond Antioch, Barnabas and Saul [Paul] would be used by God to touch and revolutionize the Gentile world. Had they stayed in Antioch, they would have missed the adventuresome apostolic life that God had designed for them. Accepting and obeying God's call thrust them forward into a life and ministry of divine purpose that radically affected the development and growth of the Church of Jesus Christ all over the Roman Empire.

Everything Paul and Barnabas had done in ministry until that time had been nothing more than preparation for what lay ahead. Although they had spent several serious years in ministry, it was simply "getting-ready time" for the ultimate call that was before them.

This is precisely how I felt when the Holy Spirit spoke to me about my new home. God has blessed our ministry immensely, but I was suddenly aware that everything that had occurred until that moment was preparation for what was about to follow. And what was about to transpire was so immense that it made everything up to that moment look minuscule. Those previous days were days of proving to learn how to be faithful. God was watching — and now that He was satisfied, He was ready to launch us into the calling He had for our lives, which was far larger than anything that Denise or I had imagined or anticipated.

Barnabas and Saul were immediately sent forth to begin their apostolic ministries, but it took me several months to really embrace what God had said. However, I did come around, and our family entered the greatest phase of our lives as a result. We have never had any regrets about leaving America behind and moving to the former USSR.

Today I want to encourage you to let the Lord reveal to you His plan for your life. It may be different from what you had previously thought. It is possible that everything you have done up until now has merely been preparation for a greater call before you. So open your heart and be careful to pay heed if the Holy Spirit affirms that He's leading you to take a new direction. It could add more fruitfulness and adventure to your life than you ever dreamed possible!

My Prayer for Today

Father, I thank You for Your predetermined plan for my life — and that You want to launch me into it as soon as I'm ready. I ask You to help me prove myself faithful where I am, so I will be prepared for the call that lies ahead of me. Help me not to be stuck in my thinking — assuming that where I am is the ultimate end of what I am called to do. I ask You to open my eyes to see that great and wonderful things lie ahead of me if I will fully surrender to You! I pray this in Jesus' name!

My Confession for Today

I confess that God knows the good plans He has for me. He is ordering my steps along His ordained path, and I am following the Holy Spirit's direction to do all He is leading me to do in preparation for God's next phase of my life. I recognize now that all I have done thus far has been preparation for the next part of His call on my life. Jesus, You said if a man is faithful in little, You will put him over much. So I declare that I will be faithful in every assignment You've given to me now, and I believe that You will promote me to the next phase when You have found me proven and ready. I declare this by faith in Jesus' name!

Questions for You to Consider

1. What are you doing right now to give yourself fully to the tasks at hand, so God will know that you are proven and ready for the job ahead of you?

   _____

   _____

   _____

   _____

   _____

   _____

2. Has God ever told you something that caught you off guard and by surprise? If so, when was that, and what did He say? Have you followed through on what He spoke to your heart?

   _____

   _____

   _____

   _____

   _____

   _____

3. Are you doing what God has told you to do right now? Are you being faithful with the call that He's given you? If God were asked this question, how would He answer about you?

_____

_____

_____

_____

_____

_____

Day 25

Machine-Gun Fire and a Cup of Tea!

> *But as many as are led by the Spirit of God, they are the sons of God.*
>
> — Romans 8:14

It was the early 1990s — a time when supernatural doors were flying open for our TV ministry in nearly every corner of the Soviet Union. But one area that remained closed was Baku, Azerbaijan. Since this was a Muslim city, I had been strongly advised not to go there to negotiate for television time. Plus, the country of Azerbaijan was in a serious military conflict at the time. But despite what people were advising me to do, I sensed a strong leading of the Holy Spirit to go there. I simply *knew* that if I would put my feet on that land, God would open doors for us to broadcast the teaching of the Bible there.

We watched the news day by day to monitor what was happening with the military developments that were largely based around the capital city of Baku

— where the largest TV tower in that part of the world was located. This tower was so huge, its signal covered not only Azerbaijan, but it reached all the way into the heart of Iran. For a door of this size to open would definitely require the supernatural grace of God — and it would also require divine courage to go there in the middle of an escalating military conflict!

A single day came when a temporary cease-fire had been declared, so we quickly purchased plane tickets for two team members and me. We called to set up an appointment with the director of the national TV station, and we raced to the airport so we could board our plane to Azerbaijan. Hours later, we landed in the capital city of Baku. After being vigorously searched at the airport, a private car picked us up and drove us directly to the broadcasting company of that nation.

When we entered the broadcasting building, we were escorted to a sitting area to wait for our meeting with the TV director. We were told that we would need to be patient because the cease-fire had been broken at almost that exact moment, and there was heavy machine-gun fighting all around the TV facility. A secretary asked us if we'd like a cup of tea, and we sat drinking our tea while we could hear gunfire at the other end of the hallway adjacent to the area where we were seated! At one point, a group of soldiers carrying machine guns ran hurriedly past us, disappearing through the door to an area outside where all the action was taking place!

Soon the door opened to the national TV director's office, and we were invited in for our scheduled appointment. To my surprise, the director was a woman. She held an unusual, very powerful position in a Muslim society. When I made my presentation about our TV programs, she responded, "Maybe you don't understand. We are a Muslim republic. Your programs can't be broadcast here. Plus, our signal reaches Tehran, and if we run your Bible teaching programs, it could offend our partners in Iran."

But this broadcasting endeavor had been on my heart a long time. So rather than take no for an answer, I insisted, "We've come a long way today. Will you please just look at one of our programs?"

The director kindly consented. It just so happened that the random program she chose to watch was part of a series on what the Bible teaches about how husbands should treat their wives. As we watched, I could see the Holy Spirit was touching her heart with answers she had been seeking for her own marriage.

When that program ended, she asked if we had Part Two of that series with us and could show it to her. By the end of the second program, the Holy Spirit had totally melted her heart. She said, "How often would you like to broadcast these programs and what price would you like to pay?"

Right before our eyes — *with machine guns firing rapid-fire in the background* — God opened a door that would not have opened if we had not had the courage to go to Baku at that critical moment in history.

That day I learned once again that it takes courage and confidence if you want to walk through a door that has never opened for anyone else. *It also takes the leading of the Holy Spirit.* It was the Holy Spirit who led us there on that very day — the day a great door flew open for the proclamation of the Gospel of Jesus Christ!

In Romans 8:14, we are promised, "But as many as are led by the Spirit of God, they are the sons of God." I want to examine this verse in today's *Sparkling Gem*.

The Greek word for "led" is the word *ago*, which simply means *to lead*. But it must also be pointed out that this word forms the root for the Greek word *agon*, which describes *an intense conflict, such as a struggle in a wrestling match* or *a struggle of the human will*.

This illustrates the fact that although the Holy Spirit wants to lead us, our human will doesn't like the idea of being led. You see, it's the nature of the flesh to want to go its own way. Thus, when we choose to walk in the Spirit and let Him dictate our lives, His leadership over us creates a struggle of our will with our flesh.

An example of this kind of intense struggle is that dangerous trip to Baku. The Spirit of God inside me was telling me, "Go *now* — there is an open door for you *today*." But the flesh ranted and raved, "You're putting your life in danger! Don't do what the Holy Spirit is telling you to do."

Maybe that's how you've been feeling about your own life. You want to obey God and be led by His Spirit, but your flesh is interested only in self-preservation and going its own way. However, as a child of God, you must learn to walk with Him and stay in your place — *behind* the Holy Spirit, following His lead. You have to defeat every fight the flesh puts up to stop you from obtaining the supernatural results the Lord wants you to have.

If you really want to live a supernatural, Spirit-led life, there is no way around it. You have to deal with your flesh! The flesh wants to control you, so you must mortify, or defeat, the flesh and allow the Holy Spirit to have His way. The struggle may seem great, but it's the only way to live a fruitful Christian life. I'm so thankful for that day many years ago when God empowered me by His Spirit and gave me the courage to get on a plane and fly to Baku. God knew what I didn't know — that a great open door was waiting for me. When we arrived and found the cease-fire had been broken, we could have turned around, gotten back on the plane, and headed home immediately. But we were *certain* the Holy Spirit was leading us. By God's grace, the fight with the flesh was won, and a great event occurred before our very eyes.

As we do the will of God in life, we must listen to natural advice, but we must never forget that the leading of the Spirit is the prime factor in yielding supernatural fruit and obtaining a heavenly outcome.

My Prayer for Today

Father, I now recognize that every time I have ever struggled to do what You asked me to do, the reason behind the struggle was that I had allowed fear and carnal reasoning to hinder me. Father, I repent for yielding to the pull of my own flesh instead of to the direction of Your Spirit. I want to live a fruitful life. Holy Spirit, right now I yield to Your strength, and I receive the courage I need to step out by faith and follow Your leading so I can obtain a heavenly outcome to the glory of God! I pray this in Jesus' Name!

My Confession for Today

I confess that I obey God and I am led by His Spirit. I put to death all self-interest and every fleshly thought to make decisions based on self-preservation. I belong to God! My life is His, and His strength is mine! I refuse to allow my flesh to stop me from obtaining the supernatural results the Lord wants me to have. I choose to do the will of God. I declare right now that in those moments when the struggle to stay on track with His plan seems great because I'm tempted to let natural reasoning pull me off course, I will not fall short but will fulfill all of the will of God without wavering! Greater is the courage of God within me than any fear that rants against my mind or any opposition that rises against me in this world! I declare this by faith in Jesus' name!

Questions for You to Consider

1. Have you ever been directed by the Holy Spirit to do something that made no sense to your natural mind? When was that? How did you respond? What was the result of your obeying what He instructed you to do?

   _____

   _____

   _____

   _____

   _____

   _____

2. Have you ever been in a place that seemed filled with danger, but God told you to be there, and it ended up bearing fruit for the Kingdom of God? When was that experience? What happened as a result of your obedience?

   _____

   _____

   _____

   _____

   _____

   _____

3. What is God asking you to do *right now* that is requiring a greater measure of spiritual fortitude for you to obey Him? Have you asked Him to give you the courage and inner strength to obey what He is asking you to do?

_____

_____

_____

_____

_____

_____

Day 26

A Divine Stream of Supernatural Revelation

> *But as it is written, Eye hath not seen, nor ear heard, neither have entered into the heart of man, the things which God hath prepared for them that love him. But God hath revealed them unto us by his Spirit: for the Spirit searcheth all things, yea, the deep things of God.*
>
> — 1 Corinthians 2:9,10

I remember one January day several years ago when I was aroused from my sleep very early in the morning, and I sensed that the Holy Spirit was awaking me because there was something He wanted to tell me. At first, I thought I was just having a difficult time sleeping, so I tried to shrug it off and go back to sleep. But the longer I lay there in my bed, the more I became aware that it was God who was stirring up my spirit. There was something He wanted to say to me.

For months preceding that time, I had been seeking answers to some very important questions about the steps we needed to take in order to fulfill the assignment God had given us. I had spent hundreds of hours thinking over the questions I faced. I had worked my ink pen over endless pages that were scrawled with my notes. Yet I couldn't find the right answer to the questions that were constantly on my mind. I had prayed and prayed about it, but it seemed that the correct answers kept evading me. Then in the early hours of that January morning, the answers *suddenly* came!

I walked back and forth in our apartment as I prayed. Finally, I went into the dining room and lay my head on the dining table to pray more earnestly. I said, *"Holy Spirit, what is it that You want to reveal to me this morning? What is it that You want to communicate to me?"*

Suddenly — and very unexpectedly — it seemed as if the spiritual realm miraculously opened, and a stream of information descended from Heaven and began to pour the answers I needed directly into my mind! As that information began surging into my mind, I *instantly* saw the solutions for which I had been seeking for so long! It was as if the Holy Spirit said, *"Let Me pull the curtains off your mind, so you can see everything you've been desiring to see. I will remove the veil of ignorance that has blinded your sight. When I do this, the ignorance will be removed and you'll instantly know every answer you've been seeking!"*

This was not the first time I'd had that experience. The Holy Spirit had revealed many things to me through the years — and I know He will continue to be my unlimited Source of divine revelation for the rest of the time I live on this earth. He will do the same for any person who genuinely seeks to know God's will for his or her life, for this is the right of every child of God.

Regarding the Holy Spirit's supernatural revelation to believers, the apostle Paul wrote, *"But as it is written, Eye hath not seen, nor ear heard, neither have entered into the heart of man, the things which God hath prepared for them that love Him. But God hath revealed them unto us by his Spirit: for the Spirit searcheth all things, yea, the deep things of God"* (1 Corinthians 2:9,10).

Paul begins this verse by talking about man's inability to understand the deep things of God by himself. It could have been translated, *"The heart of man could never dream, imagine, or conjure up the things God hath prepared for them that love Him."* The human mind, by itself, cannot fathom, even in its wildest imagination, the wonderful things God has prepared for His people! If this is so, then how can you and I ever comprehend what God has planned for *us*?

Paul tells us the answer in the above verse: "But God hath revealed them unto us by His Spirit...." This means the day of ignorance is gone! Because the Holy Spirit has come, we can now know all the things God has planned and prepared for us!

Notice that Paul says, "But God hath *revealed* them unto us by his Spirit...." The word "revealed" is the word *apokalupto*, which means *to unveil, to reveal,* or *to uncover*. It is actually a picture of *something that is veiled or hidden at the moment when its veil or covering is suddenly removed*. As a result, what was hidden for so long now comes into plain view. And God does all of this *by His Spirit* — just as He did for me on that early morning in January!

When the Holy Spirit lifts the cover and removes the veil that has blocked your view of God's plans for you, the eyes of your spirit *suddenly* see and perceive truths that were previously veiled. This is what the Bible calls a *revelation*. In one instant, everything comes into clear view, answering all your questions and giving you the direction you've been seeking for a long time.

The word *apokalupsis* suggests this meaning for First Corinthians 2:9,10:

"...God has supernaturally pulled back the veil that previously obscured your view and blocked God's plan from your sight. It was the Holy Spirit who actually carried out this operation and made all of these once-concealed things now visible to you...."

Truthfully, God gave us our brains so we could use them, and we need to learn how to use them well. But there are some things the mind alone will *never* perceive. If we are ever going to see those spiritual truths, we will have to have a spiritual experience that opens our eyes to them.

If you have been seeking answers that your mind can't find, why not go to the ultimate Source of divine revelation? God holds all the answers you seek. As you sincerely ask in faith and genuinely open your heart so the Holy Spirit can speak to you, He will tell you everything He wants you to know!

My Prayer for Today

Lord, now I understand that I've been trying to find answers I'll never discover by myself. The things I long to know can only be revealed by You, so today I ask You to pull back the veil that has concealed those things I long to understand. I know that when You get involved, my eyes will be opened and my ignorance will evaporate. I sincerely ask You in faith to speak to me and to show me those things I need to know. I pray this in Jesus' name!

My Confession for Today

I affirm that with the help of the Holy Spirit, I clearly see and understand everything the Holy Spirit wants me to know. The day of ignorance has been removed because the Holy Spirit has come to reveal the benefits Jesus has provided for me. Now I have access to the secrets that were previously hidden to my natural mind and perception. I am thankful for the Spirit's revealing work in my life, and I declare that I never have to claim ignorance again! I declare this by faith in Jesus' name!

Questions for You to Consider

1. Have you been seeking God for answers that seem elusive to you?

   _____

   _____

   _____

   _____

   _____

   _____

2. Why not make a list of the questions for which you're seeking answers?

   _____

   _____

   _____

   _____

   _____

   _____

3. Have you sincerely asked in faith for answers to your questions and then genuinely opened your heart to God so He can speak to you?

_____

_____

_____

_____

_____

_____

Day 27

A Guaranteed Way to Infuriate the Holy Spirit!

> *Do ye think that the scripture saith in vain, The Spirit that dwelleth in us lusteth to envy?*
>
> — **James 4:5**

I know you want to please the Spirit of God with your life, so today I want to tell you about something that is guaranteed *not* to please Him. By knowing this, you can avoid grieving Him and can concentrate your attention on doing those things that are sure to bring Him pleasure.

James 4:5 says, "Do ye think that the scripture saith in vain, the spirit that dwelleth in us lusteth to envy?" I want to draw your attention to the word "envy" in this verse. But first I want to back up and speak to you about the "lust" that the Holy Spirit feels for you and me.

The word "lust" is the Greek word *epipotheo,* a word that portrays *an intense desire; a craving; a hunger; an ache; a yearning for something; a longing or pining for something.* Usually this word is used to indicate an intense yearning for something that is morally wrong and sinful. But in James 4:5, this Greek word describes the intense yearning that the Holy Spirit possesses to have us entirely for Himself. Because the word *epipotheo* is used to depict the Spirit's longing to have us, it expresses the deep love and affection that the Spirit of God has for every believer.

However, James goes on to tell us that in addition to this intense yearning for us, the Holy Spirit also experiences "envy" regarding you and me. The word "envy" in James 4:5 is the Greek word *phthnos,* a word that describes *a person who is jealous about something; a person who feels rivalry or envy;* or *a person who holds a grudge because of someone else's behavior.* It also carries the idea of *ill will* and *malice.*

This word *phthnos* is the very word that would have been used to illustrate the emotions a young man experiences when he discovers his spouse is being romantically pursued by someone else. Because James uses this word to depict the Holy Spirit, we need to stop and think about what it means for a few moments.

Anger, resentment, rage, envy, jealousy — these are the emotions a man feels in such a situation. He takes this threat to his marital relationship very personally and holds a *grudge* against the pursuer. Every time the husband thinks about what that romantic bandit is trying to do, feelings of *malice* and *ill will* toward the violator rise up in his soul.

Even more significantly, a man who really loves his wife is not going to sit by and watch his wife be stolen! The envy and jealousy he feels will move him to *action* — to do everything in his power to win back his wife and permanently eliminate his competitor.

Because the husband is envious, he does all he can to see his relationship with his wife restored. All of these ideas are conveyed by the Greek word *phthnos* used in James 4:5 when the Bible tells us about the "envy" of the Holy Spirit.

One scholar says the picture contained in the Greek word phthnos could be understood this way: "*The Spirit takes it very personally when we share our lives with the world. He wants us so entirely for Himself that if the world tries to take us away, it infuriates Him. You need to know that in these cases, the Holy Spirit will not idly sit by and watch it happen. He'll do something to change the situation!*"

Not only does it infuriate the Holy Spirit when believers turn their devotion to the world, but it drives Him to intense jealousy. At this point, He will release His full rage against that unholy relationship, moving on the scene like a Divine Lover who has come to defend and rescue the relationship He holds so dear. This is something you can be sure of: If you commit more of your heart, soul, and attention to worldly things than you give to the Spirit of God, He will *not* take it lightly.

Never forget that the Holy Spirit is a Divine Lover. He is preoccupied with you. He wants to possess you totally, and He desires that your affection be set wholly on Him. That's why the Holy Spirit feels like a lover who has been robbed if you walk and talk like an unbeliever or give your life to the things of this world. He jealously desires His relationship with you to be restored. He has divine malice toward the worldliness that has usurped His role in your life.

The Holy Spirit is *not* a passive Partner. He aggressively and actively pursues you. He fiercely wants more of you. When you give part of yourself to something or someone else's control, the Holy Spirit wants to seize that part of your life and bring it back under His divine control. He even has malice toward your preoccupation with things in this natural realm.

So make your relationship with the Holy Spirit your top priority. Don't give Him a reason to feel betrayed by or envious of other things in your life that have taken His place. Get to know the Holy Spirit's voice in your spirit so He can help you set your life in order. Make sure *every* area of your life is under His loving control!

My Prayer for Today

Lord, if I ever turn my devotion to the world, please move on the scene like a Divine Lover who has come to defend and rescue that relationship You hold so dear. Help me never to forget that You are preoccupied with me and want to possess me totally. I know that You want my desires and affection to be set on You, so if I begin to walk and talk like an unbeliever and give my life to the things of this world, please nudge me and bring conviction to my heart to change. And if I refuse to listen, I ask You to please move with divine malice toward those things that have usurped Your role in my life. I pray this in Jesus' name!

My Confession for Today

I confess that I respect the Holy Spirit's presence in my life; therefore, I am careful in the way I think, the way I speak, and the way I connect with the world around me. I do not grieve the Spirit of God by allowing worldliness to become a part of my life. He fiercely wants more of me, and I want more of Him. The Holy Spirit is the top priority in my life, and I never do anything that would make Him feel wounded, grieved, or envious. I live a life that pleases Him! I declare this by faith in Jesus' name!

Questions for You to Consider

1. Is your relationship with the Holy Spirit the top priority in your life?

   _____

   _____

   _____

   _____

   _____

   _____

2. Have you allowed anything in your life to usurp the position that only the Holy Spirit should have?

   _____

   _____

   _____

   _____

   _____

3. Why not take inventory of your "love life" today, asking the Holy Spirit to show you areas in your life where you have allowed your affection to be diverted from Him to other things?

_____

_____

_____

_____

_____

_____

Day 28

What to Do When Your Spirit Is Inwardly Disturbed

> *I had no rest in my spirit, because I found not Titus my brother: but taking my leave of them, I went from thence into Macedonia.*
>
> **— 2 Corinthians 2:13**

Many years ago, I developed an uneasy feeling about a longtime member of our team who worked in a leadership position in our ministry. However, because this person had always been faithful during his years with our organization, I tried to shrug off this uneasiness and ignore what I was feeling. Naturally speaking, there was no reason for me to be suspicious of him or to question his activities. All outward signs said he was doing an excellent job; yet I kept getting a gnawing feeling in my spirit that I should no longer trust him. To put it simply, I was *deeply troubled* on the inside and knew something was *wrong*.

When an occasion would arise for this man and me to be together, I'd look deeply into his eyes when he spoke to see if I could detect whether there was something he was trying to hide. When he spoke, I'd listen carefully to his words to see if there was anything misleading in what he told me. I took notice of his gestures, trying to ascertain whether or not he was acting nervous in my presence because he had something to hide. From all outward signs, everything seemed normal — yet *inwardly* I was still extremely disturbed.

I would tell Denise, "I don't know what it is, but I sense that something is wrong with that person. Is God speaking to my spirit, or am I just being suspicious and untrusting of someone who has been faithful for a long time?" Because I could never put my finger on anything this man had done wrong, I decided that *I* was the problem — that I was being overly suspicious and needed to stop being so skeptical and wary of this devoted employee.

For the next year, I tried hard to shake off those uneasy feelings, but I just couldn't do it. Even though I couldn't identify a specific problem, I *inwardly* knew that things on the surface were not as they really seemed concerning this employee.

After a year of struggling with this issue, I discovered that this man had been acting fraudulently on many fronts. It wasn't just a case of someone doing something wrong by accident; this was purposeful wrongdoing and manipulation of the truth for his own advantage. He had been conniving and deliberately misleading. I was *shocked* when I discovered the length and breadth he had gone to deceive me and our other leaders.

By the time I made my discovery of what this employee had been doing, severe damage had already been done in that department of our organization.

But the truth is, the Holy Spirit had been warning me of the problem for a very long time. That inward uneasiness I had experienced was His warning to me to back away from this man!

God's Spirit was trying to save me from the troubles produced by this employee who was conspiring against the work of the Gospel. If I had listened to my heart and followed what I sensed on the inside, I could have avoided the pain this man tried to bring about in our lives. I praise God that when I finally made this discovery, I had the courage to take fast action and terminate this attack!

From this experience that took place so many years ago, I learned the important lesson of paying attention when my spirit is inwardly disturbed. Very often this is God's way of giving us an *alert signal* that something is not right or that something is not as it seems on the surface.

That's why you must learn to pay attention when your spirit is inwardly troubled. Set aside some time to spend with the Lord, and ask the Holy Spirit to help you quiet your mind and emotions so He can reveal to you anything you need to know about the situation. Back up and take a good look at what is happening around you, and be willing to see the truth — even if it is something you'd rather not acknowledge! If you find that everything is fine, you can then move forward with the confidence that you did your homework. But if you find out that something is wrong, you'll be thankful you listened to your spirit and slowed down so you could make this discovery in order to deal with it — for your sake and the sake of others who may be adversely affected by it!

So ask yourself these questions:

Have you ever had an inward uneasiness or a lack of peace that you later wished you hadn't ignored? Can you think of a time when the Holy Spirit tried to warn you of a problem, but you didn't listen to your heart and therefore ended up with a problem that could have been avoided? Have you discovered that God is often speaking to you when you have a lack of peace in your heart — and that He is trying to tell you to back up and slow down, to take a more cautious approach to what you are doing?

This kind of *inward disturbance* must be what Paul experienced when he came to the city of Troas and didn't find Titus waiting for him there. Although this exact event isn't recorded in the book of Acts, Paul mentioned it in his second letter to the Corinthian church. On one of his missionary journeys, Paul came to Troas, expecting to find Titus waiting for him. Paul was so taken aback that Titus wasn't there that he wrote, "I had no rest in my spirit, because I found not Titus my brother: but taking my leave of them, I went from thence into Macedonia" (2 Corinthians 2:13).

The word "rest" that Paul used in this verse comes from the Greek word *anesis*, which means *to let up*, *to relax*, *to stop being stressed*, or *to find relief*. In the Greek world, this word *anesis* could denote *the release of a bowstring that had been under great pressure*. Hence, it suggests the idea of *relief*. When used on a personal level, the word *anesis* depicts a person who has been under some type of pressure for a long time but has suddenly found a *release* from that pressure. You could say that this person has decided he is going to *shake off* and *let go of* whatever has been bothering him or the pressure he has been under.

However, Paul told us he could *not* shake off what he was inwardly feeling in his spirit. He was so *restless* or *inwardly disturbed* that he immediately left Troas and went on to Macedonia to search for his dear friend Titus. The phrase "taking my leave of them" is very strong in the Greek. It lets us know that Paul didn't take a long time to respond to this inward disturbance in his spirit; rather, he took it as a God-given signal that something wasn't right. Hence, Paul bade the believers in Troas farewell and quickly traveled into Macedonia to seek out his missing ministry friend.

Unlike my own scenario that I just related to you, the apostle Paul *listened* to his spirit. He knew that if he was *inwardly disturbed*, it could be a warning sign that something was wrong. Thus, he responded with urgency and took appropriate action when he had this kind of inner witness. How I wish I had done the same thing years ago! If I had listened to what my spirit was telling me, I could have avoided the many troubles that leader tried to create for me and for our ministry.

In light of all this, Second Corinthians 2:13 could be paraphrased: "*Regardless of how hard I tried to shake off a sense of inward disturbance, in my spirit I knew something was wrong. I tried to shake it off and let it go, but inwardly, I knew things were not right.*"

As believers, we must learn to pay attention to the lack of peace we feel in our spirits. Sometimes that lack of peace or inward disturbance is God's way of alerting us to something important or of telling us that something isn't right. God lovingly tries to spare us from problems and catastrophes. However, if we don't pay attention to the still, small voice in our hearts when the Holy Spirit tenderly speaks to us, we will end up with troubles that could have been altogether avoided or corrected before they got out of hand.

God is faithful to speak to you — but His voice can often be heard only by what you sense in your own heart. If you sense peace in your heart, it could be the Holy Spirit telling you, *"You have a green light, so you can proceed."* But if you have a lack of peace or an inward disturbance, never forget that it could be God's way of saying *"Yellow light, so proceed with caution."* Or He may even be telling you, *"Red alert! Stop! Something is wrong!"*

Don't make the mistake I made many years ago by ignoring that lack of peace in your heart. It will be far better for you if you take a little time to back up, slow down, and find out why you're feeling uneasy on the inside. If you find that everything is all right, you will then be able to move forward with assurance. But if you learn that something is *not* right, you'll be so thankful that you listened to your heart and got things in order before you proceeded any further and damage was done!

My Prayer for Today

Father, I thank You for Your Spirit, who is so faithful to alert me when things are not right. Please forgive me for the many times You tried to warn and help me, but I ignored Your voice and found myself in a mess I could have avoided. From this day forward, I am asking You to help me become more sensitive to my spirit. Help me pay attention to the peace or the lack of peace I inwardly sense so I can respond appropriately when You are trying to warn me that something isn't the way it should be. I pray this in Jesus' name!

My Confession for Today

I confess that I am sensitive to the Spirit of God. When He speaks to my heart, I quickly respond to Him and obey His instructions. I hear His voice indicating when I have God's green light to move ahead; therefore, I step out in faith. When I sense God's yellow light to move slowly and with caution, I am careful and cautious. When my spirit is inwardly disturbed and I have no peace, I know that this is God's red light — one of the ways He alerts me that something is not right. Because I am sensitive to what God is telling me in my spirit, I am able to move forward with confidence that I am not going to make a mistake! I declare this by faith in Jesus' name!

Questions for You to Consider

1. Can you think of a time when you were inwardly disturbed but you ignored it — and then later found out it was God trying to warn you about something? When was that, and what happened?

   _____

   _____

   _____

   _____

   _____

   _____

2. What did you learn from that experience when you ignored what you sensed in your spirit?

   _____

   _____

   _____

   _____

   _____

   _____

3. When you sense an inward disturbance, a lack of peace, or a restlessness in your spirit, how should you respond to it?

_____

_____

_____

_____

_____

_____

Day 29

Learning to Follow the Leader

> *For as many as are led by the Spirit of God, they are the sons of God.*
>
> — Romans 8:14

When I was a young boy, I used to play a game with my sister and childhood friends called "Follow the Leader." The rules of the game dictated that the leader had absolute authority to tell us what to do. I always wanted to be the leader, but my older sister would always end up in that coveted leadership role. The leader said what we could play, who would clean the house, and so on. We basically did *whatever* she told us to do. No wonder my older sister always wanted to be the leader!

When I think back on those playtime experiences as a boy, I am reminded of Romans 8:14, where the apostle Paul talks about following the leadership of the Holy Spirit. He wrote, "For as many as are led by the Spirit of God, they are the sons of God." In Greek, the sentence structure is actually reversed, so that it reads, "For as many as by the Spirit of God are being led, they are the sons of God." It puts the Holy Spirit at the first of the verse, and we are placed behind Him — a picture of our responsibility as children of God to "follow the Leader."

The Greek word for "led" is *ago*, which simply means *to lead*. However, I want to point out that this word is also the root for the Greek word *agon*, which describes *an intense conflict*, such as *a struggle in a wrestling match* or *a struggle of the human will*. Thus, we see that although the Holy Spirit wants to lead us, our human will doesn't like the idea of being led. The flesh always distrusts guidance or instruction given by a person in a position of authority, and it's human nature to want to call the shots and lead the way. Whether young or old, most people don't like the idea of being led. When I played "Follow the Leader" as a child, I didn't like being led by my sister and being told what to do. I'd rather have been in charge myself and called the shots as *I* saw them!

In the same way, when we make the decision to allow the Holy Spirit to dictate the course of our lives, it often produces a struggle between our will and our flesh. However, as children of God, we must learn to subdue the complaints of our flesh and stay in our place — behind the Holy Spirit as *followers*. We're not to be out front directing the Holy Spirit; we are to go *behind* Him, following His leading, direction, and guidance. The mark of a mature believer is his or her ability to sense where the Lord is leading and then to follow that leading.

The fact that the Greek word for "led" is also the root of the Greek word for *struggle* tells us that we will have to deal with our flesh as we begin to rely fully on the Holy Spirit as our Coach and Guide. Our flesh wants to control our lives, so we must say no to it and allow the Holy Spirit to have His way. Regardless of how great the struggle seems, this process of trusting the Holy Spirit's leadership is the only way to live a supernatural Christian life.

In a certain sense, we should make it our goal to be "tagalongs" to the Holy Spirit. We should continually follow along to see what He is doing, where He is going, and how He is leading — and then we should obey His leading implicitly. Just as Jesus emulated the Father's actions, we must be sensitive to the leading of the Holy Spirit and then follow His cues. In other words, we must "be led by the Spirit," which is both the responsibility and benefit of being a child of God. To become the mature Christians God wants us to be, we must have this practical relationship with the Holy Spirit.

The leading of the Holy Spirit is often subtle, taking the form of an impression or nudging in our hearts to do something. However, His leading can also be more dramatic, such as through a prophecy, dream, or vision, or simply through a voice speaking clearly to our spirits.

The truth is, learning to know the voice of the Holy Spirit and being led by Him should be one of your primary concerns as a growing, maturing child of God. It's all part of that lifelong pursuit to know Him and the power of His resurrection as you press toward the mark of the high calling in Christ Jesus!

My Prayer for Today

Heavenly Father, I want to learn how to become a "tagalong" behind the leadership of the Holy Spirit. I know You sent the Holy Spirit to be my supernatural Coach — but that His Help is only a reality to me if I choose to obey His leading. I admit that I have often struggled with obedience, and I ask You to forgive me. I really want to obey. Today I ask You to give me the strength of will and the inward surrender of heart to trust and obey the Holy Spirit and do exactly what He is trying to lead me to do. I pray this in Jesus' name!

My Confession for Today

I declare that I am tuned in to the Spirit of God and that I boldly obey whatever He instructs me to do. Fear and lack of trust do not dictate my obedience to the Holy Spirit. He is the Spirit of truth. He will never mislead me or misguide me, and I am confident of His leadership over my life. Even when I do not understand the reasons why He is leading me in a certain way, I choose to obey Him. He is the Spirit of truth. Therefore, I am confident that He is directing me into the perfect will of God for every sphere of my life. I declare this by faith in Jesus' name!

Questions for You to Consider

1. Can you truthfully say that you are a consistent "tagalong" who follows behind the Holy Spirit? Or do you find that most of the time you are out front, trying to direct Him as to what should be happening in your life?

_____

_____

_____

_____

_____

2. Have you ever experienced an inner struggle after making a decision to follow the leading of the Holy Spirit? Perhaps He nudged you to do something — or to refrain from doing something — and you found it very difficult to do so, even though you were certain it was His divine leading?

_____

_____

_____

_____

_____

3. Have you ever experienced a struggle when the Holy Spirit instructed you to witness to someone, but you found it difficult to obey? Or perhaps you sensed the Holy Spirit's leading to give a sacrificial offering, and your flesh put up a fight against His instruction in your heart. Can you think of other instances where you had to mortify your flesh in order to obey what the Holy Spirit was directing you to do or not to do?

_____

_____

_____

_____

_____

Day 30

A Different Kind of Leading

> *And when Jesus departed thence, two blind men followed him, crying, and saying, Thou Son of David, have mercy on us.... Then touched he their eyes, saying, According to your faith be it unto you.*
>
> — **Matthew 9:27,29**

Today I want to further highlight Jesus' own supernatural partnership with the Holy Spirit. It's so important to grasp the fact that Jesus depended *entirely* on the Holy Spirit's guidance during His earthly ministry as He preached and performed miracles throughout the land. And with that in mind, let's focus in on this truth: *Everything* Jesus did in His earthly ministry worked! Every single sick person He laid hands on was healed. Every demon He cast out of a possessed person left for good. Even the dead rose to His command! *His rate of success was 100 percent.*

What was the key to Jesus' success? Just this: *He never took action unless He knew the Father through His Spirit was leading Him to do so.* Jesus never attempted to heal a sick person, cast out a demon, or raise the dead without first knowing that He was doing what He saw the Father do (*see* John 5:19).

An interesting example of Jesus' spiritual partnership with the Holy Spirit can be found in the account of the two blind beggars in Matthew 9:27-31. As it is related in this passage, two beggars heard Jesus walking by them and began to cry out to Him for healing. However, instead of stopping to heal them, Jesus continued on His way without even acknowledging their presence. As a result, verse 27 states they "...followed him, crying and saying, Thou Son of David, have mercy on us." Even though they were blind and couldn't see where they were going, these beggars were determined to follow Jesus until they got His attention, and the Bible says they were "crying." This word "crying" is the Greek word *kradzo*, which means *to scream, to yell, to exclaim,* or *to cry out.* In other words, the two blind beggars were exerting every ounce of their hearts and their efforts into using their mouths to make a *sound* that would cause Jesus to turn His attention on them so they could *get Jesus' attention*!

Think about this situation for a moment. It is a very unusual depiction of Jesus. There were two blind men who desperately wanted to be healed and were crying out to get Jesus' attention. Yet instead of stopping to help them, Jesus just continued on His way as though they weren't even there. Still they pursued Him relentlessly. Groping along in their darkness, the blind men screamed, yelled, and cried out at the top of their lungs: *"Have mercy on us! Have mercy on us! Have mercy on us!"* There was no way that Jesus didn't hear their cries, but He didn't stop to acknowledge their existence.

In Matthew 9:28, we see that these blind beggars followed Him all the way to the house where He was staying and continued to cry out, *"Son of David, have mercy on us!"* Finally, Jesus came outside and addressed them, "Do you believe that I can do this?" They answered, "Yea, Lord." Then Jesus touched their eyes and said, "According to your faith be it unto you," and their eyes were immediately opened (v. 30).

Although this passage of Scripture relates the story of a mighty healing miracle, it perplexed me for many years. Why didn't Jesus acknowledge them? Why didn't He immediately turn to heal them when He learned of their blind condition? What were the reasons behind His hesitation?

After meditating on this subject, I came to a realization. The only answer possible is that Jesus evidently did not sense the leading of the Holy Spirit in that moment to restore sight to those men. Otherwise, He would have stopped to do it, because as Jesus stated in John 5:19, He did only whatever He saw the Father do, regardless of His own inclinations. The good news is that those men were able to use their own faith to be healed, anyway, and their sight was miraculously restored. In fact, it is almost as if Jesus told them, "You are going to have to receive this on your own. Be it unto you according to your own faith."

Usually we think of the Holy Spirit leading us *to do* something; however, in the case of the two blind beggars, Jesus was led to do *nothing*. If He had been led to heal them, He would have healed them immediately, just as He had done on countless other instances.

So often we get caught up in following our own plans and miss out entirely on what the Holy Spirit is attempting to do and say through us. We get the ball rolling on a project, and then after our program is already well underway, we pray and ask God to bless what we have initiated — assuming it was His will in the first place. No wonder we often have such poor results! We must learn to let the Holy Spirit lead us just as He led Jesus.

If the Holy Spirit leads us to action, we should act — but if there is no leading, we should *do nothing*. Sometimes doing nothing is the right thing to do!

I can think of many instances when I saw something that was a good idea — something I thought someone should do — but I felt no unction to do it, and knew I would be wrong if I did it. In those cases, someone else had to use his or her faith to get it done, and ultimately that task was completed — *but by someone else, not me.*

I'm sure that when Jesus first saw those two blind beggars, He felt tugged by compassion to immediately reach out and heal them. However, He did only what He saw the Father doing, and He initiated nothing without first being led by the Holy Spirit. *That is why His success rate was 100 percent!*

Instead of jumping into action every time you see a need, learn to put on the brakes, stop yourself for a moment, and wait until the Holy Spirit speaks clearly to your heart. It may seem as though this way of doing things takes longer, but the end results will be far more rewarding and long-lasting if you adopt Jesus' approach and rely on the guidance of the Holy Spirit rather than just going with your own preplanned program. *You'll find that your success rate will increase dramatically!*

My Prayer for Today

Father, I ask You to help me learn to be keenly sensitive to the leading of the Holy Spirit — paying attention not just to when I should take action, but also to when I should do nothing. I've never thought about the Holy Spirit leading me to do nothing, but I can see that sometimes it is not His will for me to take action because He wants to work in a different way, at a different time, or through someone else. I admit that I've often assumed I knew what the Holy Spirit wanted me to do and then acted presumptuously without even praying. Now I understand why my success rate has not been as high as I desire. Help me be like Jesus — taking action only when the Holy Spirit is leading. I pray this in Jesus' name!

My Confession for Today

I confess that I am led by the Holy Spirit and that I refuse to jump into action simply because I see something that needs to be done or because I am aware of a need that should be met. I put on the brakes; I listen; and I wait for the Holy Spirit to speak to my heart. Because I take action when He speaks to me and I do exactly what He tells me to do, I experience His supernatural power and supernatural results in my life. I confess that I will endeavor to do things the way Jesus did — doing only what He knew was being initiated by the Father and the Holy Spirit! I declare this by faith in Jesus' name!

Questions for You to Consider

1. Can you think of an instance when you assumed you were supposed to take action, but in actuality, the Holy Spirit had not led you to do anything at all?

   _____

   _____

   _____

   _____

   _____

2. Can you recall other times in the four gospels when Jesus didn't heal someone? What do you learn about being led by the Holy Spirit by studying those examples?

   _____

   _____

   _____

   _____

   _____

3. Have you ever done something out of compulsion? Perhaps you thought this task needed to be done and it cost you a lot, but ultimately it produced no results. As you look back on that experience, what did you learn from it?

_____

_____

_____

_____

_____

_____

Day 31

Do Not Grieve the Holy Spirit!

And grieve not the Holy Spirit of God, whereby ye are sealed unto the day of redemption.

— Ephesians 4:30

Many years ago, when I first studied the word "grieve" in Ephesians 4:30, I ran to my bookshelf and pulled out my Greek New Testament to discover exactly what the word "grieve" meant. I found that this word was taken from the Greek word *lupete*. This surprised me, because the word *lupete* is from the word *lupe*, which denotes a *pain* or *grief* that can only be experienced between two people who deeply love each other.

This word *lupe* would normally be used to picture a husband or wife who has discovered his or her mate has been unfaithful. As a result of this unfaithfulness, the betrayed spouse is *shocked, devastated, hurt, wounded,* and *grieved* because of the pain that accompanies unfaithfulness.

This tells us, first of all, that the relationship that exists between us and the Holy Spirit is precious! The Holy Spirit is deeply in love with us. Just as someone in love thinks about, dreams of, and cherishes the one he loves, the Holy Spirit longs for us, thinks about us, desires to be close to us, and wants to reveal Himself to us.

But when we act like the world, talk like the world, behave like the world, and respond the same way the world does, we cause the Spirit of God to feel shock, hurt, and grief. You see, when we deliberately do what is wrong, we drag Him right into the mire of sin with us, because He lives in us and goes wherever we go.

The Holy Spirit convicted us of sin and brought us to Jesus; then He indwelt us, sanctified us, empowered us, and faithfully remains alongside to help us. So when we deliberately enter into sin, it *grieves* Him. Just as a husband or wife would feel who has just discovered that his or her spouse has committed adultery, the Holy Spirit is *shocked* when we dishonor His presence in our lives.

One scholar has translated Ephesians 4:30 in the following way: "*Stop deeply wounding and causing such extreme emotional pain to the Spirit of God, by whom you have been sealed until the day of your redemption.*"

We need to realize how precious the Holy Spirit is in our lives and honor Him by making sure we live holy and upright lives. If our behavior has been wrong, we should confess our sin and receive cleansing by the blood of Jesus so we can be restored to fellowship with the Spirit of God.

So before you get started with your daily duties today, stop and ask, *"Holy Spirit, is there anything in my life that causes You grief? If there is, please reveal it to me so I can change."*

My Prayer for Today

Lord, I ask You to forgive me for allowing attitudes and actions in my life that are dishonoring to You. I want to please You more than ever before, so I ask You to help me recognize those negative things in my life that cause You pain. Help me to permanently walk free of them. From the depths of my heart, I thank You for all You have done inside me. Starting right now, I want to live every moment of my life with the intent to please You and to never cause You grief again. I pray this in Jesus' name!

My Confession for Today

Starting today, I make the choice to walk away from everything in my life that is displeasing and desecrating to the Holy Spirit's presence within me. I walk away from every negative thought, word, and deed that has tried to operate in me and that is dishonoring to Him. I turn the other direction to walk a new walk and talk a new talk that shows respect and love for the Spirit of God who dwells inside me. I declare this by faith in Jesus' name!

Questions for You to Consider

1. Are there any wrong attitudes or actions in your life that grieve the Holy Spirit? If so, write them down and then pray about them.

_____

_____

_____

_____

_____

2. Are there any relationships in your life that have a negative effect on your relationship with the Lord?

_____

_____

_____

_____

3. For you to get right and stay right with God, what changes do you need to make in your life?

_____

_____

_____

_____

_____

_____

About the Author

Rick Renner is a highly respected Bible teacher and leader in the international Christian community. He is the author of a long list of books, including the bestsellers *Dressed To Kill* and *Sparkling Gems From the Greek 1* and *2,* which have sold millions of copies in multiple languages worldwide. Rick's understanding of the Greek language and biblical history opens up the Scriptures in a unique way that enables his audience to gain wisdom and insight while learning something brand-new from the Word of God. Rick and his wife, Denise, have cumulatively authored more than 40 books that have been distributed worldwide.

Rick is the overseer of the Good News Association of Churches, founder of the Moscow Good News Church, pastor of the Internet Good News Church, and founder of Media Mir. He is the president of GNC (Good News Channel) — the largest Russian-speaking Christian satellite network in the world, which broadcasts the Gospel 24/7 to countless Russian-speaking viewers worldwide via multiple satellites and the Internet. Rick is the founder and president of RENNER Ministries in Broken Arrow, Oklahoma, and host to his TV program, also seen around the world in multiple languages. Rick leads this amazing work with Denise — his wife and lifelong ministry partner — along with their sons and committed leadership team.

Contact RENNER Ministries

For further information about RENNER Ministries, please contact the office nearest you, or visit the ministry website at:

www.renner.org

ALL USA CORRESPONDENCE:

RENNER Ministries
1814 W. Tacoma St.
Broken Arrow, OK 74012

Phone: 800-742-5593

Or 1-800-RICK-593

Email: **renner@renner.org**

Website: **www.renner.org**

MOSCOW OFFICE:

RENNER Ministries
PO Box 789 101000
Moscow, Russia

Phone: +7 (495) 727-1470

Email: **blagayavestonline@ignc.org**

Website: **www.ignc.org**

RIGA OFFICE:

RENNER Ministries
Unijas 99
Riga LV-1084
Latvia

Phone: +371 67802150

Email: **info@goodnews.lv**

OXFORD OFFICE:

RENNER Ministries
Box 7, 266 Banbury Road
Oxford OX2 7DL, England

Phone: +44 1865 521024

Email: **europe@renner.org**

Books by Rick Renner

Apostles & Prophets

Build Your Foundation*

Chosen by God*

Christmas — The Rest of the Story

Dream Thieves*

Dressed To Kill*

The Holy Spirit and You*

How To Keep Your Head on Straight in a World Gone Crazy*

How To Receive Answers From Heaven!*

Insights on Successful Leadership*

Last-Days Survival Guide*

A Life Ablaze*

Life in the Combat Zone*

A Light in Darkness, Volume One
Seven Messages to the Seven Churches series

The Love Test*

No Room for Compromise, Volume Two
Seven Messages to the Seven Churches series

*Paid in Full**

*The Point of No Return**

*Repentance**

*Signs You'll See Just Before Jesus Comes**

*Sparkling Gems From the Greek Daily Devotional 1**

*Sparkling Gems From the Greek Daily Devotional 2**

*Spiritual Weapons To Defeat the Enemy**

*Ten Guidelines To Help You Achieve Your Long-Awaited Promotion!**

Testing the Supernatural

365 Days of Increase

365 Days of Power

*Turn Your God-Given Dreams Into Reality**

*Unlikely — Our Faith-Filled Journey to the Ends of the Earth**

*Why We Need the Gifts of the Spirit**

*The Will of God — The Key to Your Success**

*You Can Get Over It**

---

*Digital version available for Kindle, Nook, and iBook.

Note: Books by Rick Renner are available for purchase at: **www.renner.org**

Equipping Believers to Walk in the Abundant Life

John 10:10b

Connect with us for fresh content and news about forthcoming books from your favorite authors...

Facebook @ HarrisonHousePublishers

Instagram @ HarrisonHousePublishing

www.harrisonhouse.com

My Journal

_____
_____
_____
_____
_____
_____
_____
_____
_____
_____
_____
_____
_____
_____
_____
_____
_____
_____
_____
_____
_____

My Journal

My Journal

My Journal

My Journal

My Journal

My Journal

My Journal

My Journal

My Journal

_____

_____

_____

_____

_____

_____

_____

_____

_____

_____

_____

_____

_____

_____

_____

_____

_____

_____

_____

_____

_____

_____

_____

_____

My Journal

_____
_____
_____
_____
_____
_____
_____
_____
_____
_____
_____
_____
_____
_____
_____
_____
_____
_____
_____
_____

My Journal

_____
_____
_____
_____
_____
_____
_____
_____
_____
_____
_____
_____
_____
_____
_____
_____
_____
_____
_____
_____
_____
_____
_____
_____
_____
_____
_____
_____